NOT VERY
INTELLIGENT
DESIGN
3

-

GOD
AND THE
HUMAN BRAIN

NOT VERY INTELLIGENT DESIGN

3

-

God and the Human Brain

by
Neel Ingman

ABOUT THE AUTHOR

Neel Ingman is an independent blogger who is almost universally unknown for publishing his conversations with God and the Pope, along with related bits and pieces at neelingman.com.

He also writes books like this one and puts videos on YouTube. Go to YouTube, write Neel Ingman in the search bar and voila.

In other words,

check out

neelingman.com

or go to

youtube.com/@neelingman

Version 1.1

First Publication, 2023

Palaceno House
Auckland
New Zealand

Not Very Intelligent Design 3 : God and the Human Brain

ISBN   978-0-473-70119-2

neelingman.com

NotVeryIntelligentDesign.com

kneelingman.com

Available from Amazon.com

CONTENTS

TRIGGER WARNING

This book was triggered by the books Not Very Intelligent Design, and Not Very Intelligent Design Too : Planet Earth. It's not the only thing that was triggered by those books. Some persons of faith were triggered to write scathing reviews, saying they were unscientific, shallow, subjective, and worst of all, vulgar.

This one is too. Even worse, it lurches further into hyperbole and straight-out fiction.

Hopefully it's also funny and honest. At least more intellectually honest than a creationist who claims to be offended by the idea of something being unscientific.

If you're the sort of person who gets angry when your beliefs are challenged or threatened by simple, easy-to-comprehend concepts that your faith can't deal with, don't read this book.

If language sometimes used by footballers and politicians upsets your delicate sensibilities, don't read this book.

If you're perturbed by observations regarding serious or scientific matters that are neither serious nor scientific, don't read this book.

You've been warned. To go ahead and read it, perhaps using

it as a tool for self-flagellation, is not only unwise, it may also lead you unto the temptation of bearing false witness against it for being exactly what it purports to be. Seriously, if you're any of the above types, don't read it. It's not for you. You'll hate it.

To everybody else, happy reading. I hope you enjoy it.

A note to Christians
(aka Trigger Warning 2)

Christians have been very upset with the first two books in this series. They hate it being pointed out that if God created everything he didn't do a very good job.

But God himself admitted that he did a lousy job. It says so in the Bible.

Humans were sinners. They needed to be fixed. God's creation needed heavenly recalls and remedial work, in order to function as God wished. His genocide of Humanity 1.0 in the Great Flood clearly failed to have the desired outcome as Humanity 2.0 still needed fixing.

God decided to beget the bejeebus out of Mary and then wait for nine months and then wait for a couple of decades for his only begotten son to grow up and start performing underwhelming miracles in an attempt to fix up the botched job he'd made of trying to create a perfect, sinless creature, supposedly in his own image.

However, he didn't try very hard to create a sinless creature because he deliberately introduced humanity to sin, or sin to humanity, courtesy of a talking snake. So what did he want? Humans to be sinless? Fine, leave the snake out of the garden. But no, he created sin so that he could then threaten us with eternal torture. And make out like it's all our fault when he supposedly created everything. The God of the Bible is arguably the first pathologically abusive father figure in recorded history. "Now look what you made me do." It's lucky there was no Mrs God or devout Christian men would have an even better excuse to beat their wives as well as their children.

Of course, as mentioned above, the enforced conception of the sweet baby Jesus wasn't the first time God had unsuccessfully tried a do-over on account of stuffing things up. (Sidebar - Maybe we should cut the guy a bit of slack because the creative process pretty much always involves modifications and improvements. I don't know of anybody that gets it right the first time but then again God does make some pretty big claims of perfection, omniscience and omnipotence and all that, so fuck 'im.)

God's most famous attempt to fix his creative shortcomings was the Great Flood featuring Noah's couples-only cruise ship. God apparently thought that perpetrating the largest possible act of genocide on planet Earth was consistent with his claim to be a loving and caring father figure. And it wasn't just humans that he murdered by drowning. He supposedly killed every single living thing on the face of the earth except for those who made it aboard the Annihilation Princess.

(Sidebar - Is it really reasonable to think that humans are God's chosen species when we're the ones who get slaughtered and threatened with eternal damnation, yet fish were given 70 percent of the planet with no strings attached? Until we learnt how to fish that is. Also, oceans are pretty much exempt from storms and other forms of natural disaster, and the temperatures in any given ocean habitat remain constant within a few degrees year round. Nowhere on the surface of the planet has such a benign environment for the creatures that live there.)

Instead of flooding the whole planet and getting a pair of penguins and a pair of polar bears to walk to the Middle East, couldn't he have just waved his hand, cleared the planet of living things and started again? Why not? What rule in the world of miracles and fantasy precludes that? He's theoretically more powerful than all the Marvel heroes, Harry Potter, and all the wizards and dragons in Mordor, Westeros and Essos put together. What part of his omnipotence wasn't powerful enough? Why did he choose to subject all the animals and humans to the horror of death by drowning rather than make them painlessly disappear?

Were there other times God supposedly tried to fix things he'd messed up? Meaning humans. I seem to recall that fixing us was his excuse for slaughtering whole cities or all the firstborn boys or some such bullshit, but at this point I don't care. All that would provide would be additional evidence that God's attempt to create a perfect creature in his own image was about as successful as Frankenstein's. Why'd he let that snake into the Garden of Eden? Why'd he make it talk? Mysterious. Fantastical. Nonsensical.

So, dear Christian friends, please read the Trigger Warnings of which this is the second. They are easy to find. If you get upset because you ignored the Trigger Warnings you only have yourself to blame. In fact, why are you still here? There was a Trigger Warning on the previous page for Chrissakes.

A note on sex, gender and pronouns

There's nothing in this book (apart from this page) about gender issues, pronouns and the like. That's not what this is about. I haven't paid enough attention to those issues to have a position on them. What I do believe is that every human should be treated equally and with respect (at least until such time as they reveal themselves to be a serial killer, rapist, Nazi or similar).

If there's something in this book that offends you, just take a breath, lighten up, relax, and have a guilty giggle. If you can't do that, you may as well read no further. This book will make no sense to those without a sense of humour.

At the time of the creation of gods in the consciousness of humankind, men and women would surely have had similar thoughts on the matter, but women were not empowered in any way back then so if they did express thoughts about gods they would have been ignored or possibly beaten for getting uppity. That's how things were back in the day when a man got to be the boss on account of the size of his muscles, rather than the muscle he could buy on account of the size of his bank account.

Besides, women should be okay with sitting this one out because, in the whole sorry history of the creation of gods and religions, there really hasn't been anything to be proud of. In fact, if I were a woman I'd adopt the position that women are much smarter than men because they were not involved in all the bullshit involved in inventing gods.

Pretty much all religions have a history of being misogynistic to varying degrees, from the extreme psycho, total domination model to a milder version, in which you can't be a priest and the church will tell you what you can and can't do with your body. Any easing of the inbuilt misogyny has been due to modern secular pressure rather than any enlightenment arising within the holy ones themselves.

Whether the holy men actually believe the nonsense they made up or just cynically used it for their own ends is unclear, but it probably involves both. Extreme narcissists who become cult leaders often seem to start believing in their own godliness.

This book contains generalisations. Often sweeping ones. But we all know (except for those who don't) that there are always exceptions to everything, so before you get upset with my generalisations and start thinking "not all" or "not everybody", remember that I always mean you should take that automatic exception stuff into account. Except for when I'm making an exception.

Focus and depth of field

When you decide to take a decent look at something, you must, whether or not you're conscious of doing so, decide how closely you want to look. Or in fact how closely you need to look, to find the answers that are useful or appropriate to your enquiry.

Let's say we're looking for intelligent life on another planet. If we use a home telescope we might not even find the planet, let alone be able to examine it. If we were to land a machine on the planet equipped with a powerful microscope, we might be able to examine molecular structures, but if that was the only instrument on board the lander, we'd be unable to detect an elephant if one were to walk by.

If you look at a close-up picture of a small part of a tree trunk, you have no way of knowing whether that tree is in the middle of a forest or is the only tree for a thousand miles. Or even if it's a big tree or a small one. Look even closer and you won't even know if it's a tree or something else entirely.

If you're too far away you can't see enough, but if you're too close, you can't see enough. Not a typo.

This book will attempt to look at the subject without a microscope or a telescope. It will not deliberately obfuscate or attempt to seem profound by pretending there's a need to analyse the meaning of the word "the". It will discuss things as they appear in a standard human depth of field, using plain language and hopefully from the point of view of someone with reasonable human vision. And no blinkers.

People have said that my previous books have been shallow and unserious. Fair comment. They are. Deliberately so. I see no point in attempting a detailed and scholarly examination of a thing that is so obviously deeply flawed. Although that's not quite correct. When something is flawed there's an implication that there may be other parts that are not flawed. Which isn't the case with the Bible and the whole God myth. The whole thing is fictional nonsense from start to finish.

A degree in theology is as useful for increasing one's knowledge of facts, truth and reality as a degree in Mickey Mouseology.

Genesis is no more useful as an explanation of the creation of planet Earth than a four-year-old's explanation of how he built a jumbo jet.

On the first day, I went out to get some jelly. I found it at the shop and brought it home. And it was good.

On the second day, I made the inside of the plane. I made the seats and the windows and the toilets. All made out of the special jelly. And I looked at it and it was good.

On the third day, I made the outside. And the paint. And I painted it. And it looked good.

On the fourth day, I made the engines. And they were good.

On the fifth day, I made the wings. I made the steering wheel too.

On the sixth day, I got in the plane and made it fly. The reason it flies is that it's all made of magic flying jelly.

On the seventh day I rested.

A fictional child who may have written a piece something like that about the creation of an aeroplane would have understood as much about aircraft engineering as the person who wrote the Book of Genesis understood about planet Earth and our solar system. Absolutely nothing.

A person who had actually built an aeroplane would be able to explain why their plane flies and could write a description of the process that would require no clarification of context or interpretation of hidden meanings. It would make sense. Genesis does not make sense because it was written by someone who had absolutely no knowledge or understanding of his subject matter. It reads like a book review written by a child who didn't read the book.

The discussion of whether God exists is far too often bogged down in semantics. Looking for truth in the Bible involves inventing context to try to make sense of nonsense and looking for hidden meanings where there are none. Expeditions to find Noah's Ark are as useful as trying to find out whether the above-referenced four-year-old lived near Kitty Hawk and whether he'd ever met Wilbur or Orville.

To delve deeper and dissect every sentence in the Bible has no value at all. It's just a waste of time. Unless of course you are in the business of making money from the Bible. As millions of people are.

Unfortunately, making money out of writing about the Bible pretty much involves pretending that you believe in it. So that minimises my chances of making a buck out of this book. It's a good thing that writing about the ridiculousness of the Bible can be quite good fun.

This book resembles the human brain (at least my human brain) in the way that it attempts to be organised in its discussion of the main topic, but it often wanders off, gets side-tracked, spends too much time on unimportant things, just because they're amusing, and doesn't treat the serious and important stuff seriously or in any sort of depth.

I know people who have spiritual beliefs or leanings that don't follow any mainstream religion, which is fine by me. Why not, it's entirely harmless. Unlike the big religious organisations which are the opposite. If people want to believe that God is in the trees and the clouds and the birds and the bees, that's fine by me. Hell, I've even seen him there a few times myself, with the assistance of LSD.

That's not the god this book's about. This is about the one in the Bible.

INTRODUCTION

Time is a great healer. The Romans, according to one major work of historical fantasy, disliked the things a bloke called Jesus said so much that they nailed him to a cross in an attempt to kill him. We can assume it was the things he said and did that got right up their noses because he was almost certainly incapable of writing anything down. Even if he was the only literate woodworker of his time, nothing he might have written was deemed to be worth preserving, as those who wrote the tales of his life, some decades later, never mentioned any such writings.

Not only have no writings by Jesus ever been found, but there are also no contemporaneous mentions of Jesus in any written records by anybody else. Even though the Romans were great record keepers, the great majority of the records of their time in that vicinity have not survived. Many things cannot be disproved, but proof of the actual existence of Jesus in the real world does not exist.

Anyway, some years after killing him, or not, the Romans had a change of heart and decided to make the life and times of the Jesus a thing to celebrate. It also happened to be a thing they could use to maintain control of the proletariat. So they embraced a cult that had been started in his honour, and by dint of imperial grunt, transformed it into a quasi-govern-mental powerhouse, also known as the Roman Catholic Church. This happened about 350 years after the Jesus went to heaven or wherever, and to get an idea of how much they actually knew about him by then, try to imagine finding out information about someone who lived 350 years ago if you didn't have the internet or libraries or books. Or if the official records from that time did not contain so much as a single reference to the person in question. The only record of the Jesus' supposed existence was a collection of works of hearsay (not to be confused with heresy) and creative writing, but there was no way to fact-check anything in those stories.

About 1500 years after their failed attempt to kill the Jesus, the Romans were in the process of building huge temples to glorify his purported existence and consolidate their power. They were building them everywhere they could and, logically enough, they built some seriously magnificent ones where the bosses lived.

Pope Sixtus the Fourth, in honour of himself, commissioned an interior decorator named Michelangelo to paint the ceiling of the Sistine Chapel. During the course of his engagement, it must have become very apparent to Michelangelo that he was much smarter than Pope the Sith or any of the Cardinals and Bishops he spoke to, so he could afford to take a few liberties with his artistic creation.

With this in mind, he painted an impressively ambiguous panel, one of nine on the chapel ceiling, called the Creation of Adam.

The Creation of Adam

Most depictions of God show the exalted one riding a cloud, or in some other way being above the real world, which is very much beneath him. Therefore he's also way, way above the underworld. The place where the devil lives.

Yet Michelangelo depicted God at the same level as Adam.

If Adam were to show enough respect to interrupt his decadently relaxed repose and sit up, his head would be at least level with God's. If he stood, Adam would tower over God and his encapsulated entourage of mystery chums. In fact, Adam's fun trumpet would be approximately aligned with God's face, albeit not quite as in-yer-face as Eve cops just two panels away in The Fall and Expulsion from Paradise, where Adam's johnson is within an impromptu erection of popping at least the tip into her right aural canal.

There's some speculation that the woman entrapped in God's left elbow in The Creation of Adam may be Eve or the Virgin Mary, though her eyes indicate that she may be a chess prodigy.

At the point where the protagonists' fingertips almost meet, Adam's relaxed, almost limp wrist is slightly above God's rigid one. Their bodies are the same size, although Adam's shoulders are broader but God's flowing robes preclude the possibility of a dick-measuring contest.

And then there's the bloody great elephant in the room. The elephant that Michelangelo painted with all the cheek and humour of an ancient Banksy. God's cocoon of babes, angels and other hangers-on are all contained in a shape that resembles the cross-section of the human brain, complete with the frontal lobe, optic chiasm, brain stem, pituitary gland, and the major sulci of the cerebrum. It is a depiction of anatomical detail that Michelangelo correctly guessed would elude the comprehension of all the ecclesiastical brain power that he was ever likely to encounter.

To go with the ambiguity of the visual representation, so is the title of the panel, both in English and Italian, and maybe in Latin too, though Latin gets picky about such things so maybe not.

Creation of Adam. Creazione di Adamo.

That can mean the creation of someone called Adam, or equally, a creation by someone called Adam. Either God created Adam. Or Adam created God.

Michelangelo's depiction of God and his angels or cherubs or whatever, all huddled inside the confines of a human brain is pretty easy to interpret as meaning that's the place where Michelangelo thought God existed and by extension, that's where he was created.

Some say that Michelangelo was a devout believer, but what choice did he have if he wanted the decorating gig? Or even just to continue living. It was a time when the Catholic

Church didn't stand for any heretical nonsense. The Spanish Inquisition was just getting started, having been on the rampage for a mere thirty years or so with another few hundred years ahead of it, and it was a hundred years before Galileo was tried by the Roman Catholic Inquisition for daring to suggest that his scientific observations more closely reflected reality than did the holy word. They didn't mess about with non-believers or non-compliers and Mike Angelo was no fool.

The equality of Adam and God in *The Creation of Adam*, the ambiguity of the title and especially the image itself, really does seem to warrant some kind of investigation.

Also worthy of reflection is why God supposedly created Adam from nothing, or dust, or mud, or whatever then when it came to creating Eve he needed a rib from Adam, but when it came to creating Jesus he needed to impregnate a virgin against her consent. Mysterious ways.

It's often said that the Bible should not be taken literally, which is a handy excuse for those who wish to control the interpretation of God's word for his flock. This book generally prefers to take the Bible as written, because when one critiques an interpretation, it's neither fair nor useful. Like saying Beethoven was a terrible composer because of the way the drunk man hammering away on an old upright piano outside the supermarket "interprets" his music.

Let's take the story of the Garden of Eden for example. In which Eve was charmed by a talking snake and tricked into eating an apple. What's this story really about? Temptation and lust, obviously. It doesn't take much imagination to replace the euphemisms with what the writer was really trying to say. When Eve caught sight of Adam's manhood, she started to have strange feelings and did not want to look away. Adam noticed her transfixed gaze and started to move his hips like Elvis, the jiggling motion of his free willy causing it to expand exponentially as his eyes ran up and down Eve's naked body.

Adam smiled at Eve, "How do you like them apples?" he quipped, as he cupped his nuts in one hand.

"They look pretty ripe to me", she giggled. "I wouldn't mind a taste."

Was that a wilfully dishonest take on the story? Perhaps. But when you think about it, what was more likely to lead Eve down the path to wanton sexual promiscuity with every man she could find? A talking viper, or the sight of Adam's mighty phallus, rising like a snake charmer's cobra from his unkempt bush?

This book is called God and the Human Brain so it would seem logical to start by looking at God, but things that seem logical are often not so, given how the human brain works.

And besides, anything that is observed is affected by the observer, whether it's a pre-existing bias when listening to a politician, or the position of the observer when listening to the sound of a motorcycle. The pitch of the engine either rises, falls or stays constant depending on whether the observer is in front of an approaching machine, behind a receding machine or sitting on the machine.

So it would be unwise to jump right in and start with the analysis of God, without first having a look at how the observer is likely to influence the observation. So -

In Part One we shall examine the brains of Adam's progeny as the creation of God.

In Part Two we shall examine God as the creation of the brains of Adam's progeny.

In the conclusion we shall evaluate whether the exercise was in any way worth the effort.

Spoiler - it's highly unlikely to convince anyone of anything they didn't already believe, or at least suspect, but hopefully it'll be entertaining enough to make for an enjoyable journey. So let's go.

Part One

starring

The Human Brain

as

The Creation of God

An Unfortunate Paradox

The main thing that sets humans apart from other creatures is our brains. We have the ability to think about things in abstract ways that other species may only dream about.

Lots of humans are pretty good at a couple of different types of intellectual endeavour. One of those things is studying the world we live in and coming up with explanations or theories about how it all works, and then perhaps designing useful things arising from the understanding of those theories. The other thing is creating stuff straight out of our imaginations, or, more often, as time goes by, creating new stuff inspired by other things previously created.

Both of these things are quite useful. One of them is called science and the other is called art.

When scientists question a scientific theory, they do it in a way that causes them to re-examine the evidence and the reasoning of the theory, and they'll often come up with a new consensus as a result. Such consensus isn't a compromise, or a negotiated settlement, or the decree of an authority figure, it's the best explanation of things as currently understood. (There'll always be exceptions where pride and professional jealousy step in and mess things up of course.) As a result of intelligent minds searching for verifiable, testable results, science has made our lives unrecognisably better than it was a few hundred years ago, with thousands of scientific discoveries from plumbing to electricity, from motorised carts to aircraft.

Art is valuable in terms of enlightening and explaining the human condition. Stories and songs can illustrate complex issues and help us see things from different perspectives. We're good at making shit up. The problem with the shit we make up, as opposed to the scientific theories mentioned above, is that the shit that we make up can't be examined, subjected to experiment or testing, and can be neither verified nor disproved. This is not a problem when the creator of a work of fiction presents it as fiction, but when the creator claims his fiction is true, all sorts of nonsense may ensue. Because despite being good at making up fiction, we are utterly useless at discerning the difference between fact and fiction. At least most of us are.

Our default setting is to take things at face value, which makes movies and TV shows so much fun to watch. We can suspend our disbelief so easily that we dive right into well-told stories, leaving behind the withering burden of the reality of the daily drudgery of human existence, giving it no further thought until the show's over. Provided it's well crafted. And provided your life is not so hellish that momentary mental escape is impossible.

I rate any movie a ten out of ten if I've not once looked at my watch or thought about where I am or who I am. Sometimes I walk out of a movie and I'm surprised to see where I am and the fact that it's broad daylight. Not because

I expected it to be night but because I had no expectations at all. I'd been in the world of the movie. A bit like waking up in a hotel room and taking a moment to figure out what country you're in. It's a brilliant feeling. Slightly scary but mostly exciting.

The thing that makes humans intellectually superior to all other animals is our ability to explain things that are complex and abstract. The paradox may be that it is precisely because we are so good at making shit up that makes us so poor at recognising shit that other humans made up.

Or even that we made up ourselves. My day job a few years back was writing TV drama. One day I was reading a script I'd written a few years earlier that was a drama based on factual events. The script contained fictional elements necessary to make it work as a dramatic story. Even though I'd made up the fictional bits, in a few instances I could not remember, or tell, which bits were fiction and which were factual.

Another example. A friend who knew I was writing for a TV cop show at the time asked me what I was currently working on. I outlined the plot of the episode to him. (Which I didn't mind doing as it can often help to verbally tell a story to see how well it's working.) When I finished he asked if it was a true story or if I'd made it up. He'd seen a few episodes of the show and knew the show was fiction. I'd never hinted

NOT VERY INTELLIGENT DESIGN THREE

that the story I'd just told him was anything but fiction. Yet he still thought it might be true. He's no fool. It's just how we are.

We make shit up and then we believe it.

One of the main reasons to think that God is the creation of man is the predisposition of humans to make shit up and then believe it. To believe shit that other people have made up when there is no verifiable evidence. Verifiable is an important word in that sentence. As is evidence. Humans will often dive into believing things where absolutely no evidence exists.

Homeopathy for example. Essential oils. Snake oil.

Things such as Bigfoot, aliens, the Loch Ness monster, fairies at the bottom of the garden, scary men or monsters under the bed of a child, microchipped vaccines, ghosts of many varieties, and so on. There is "evidence" for all of those things, but none of it is verifiable. Or even vaguely plausible. Except for ghosts who live in the afterlife and who are happy to chat, but only if there's a medium-rare charlatan there to clip the ticket.

The unsubstantiated evidence for some examples above can be found in comic books and other publications. The unsubstantiated evidence for the existence of God is in the Bible. The Bible exists. That's a fact. The Bible exists in many different versions and translations. That's also a fact. The stories it contains are many and varied but not verifiable.

We all know people who believe in some or all of that crazy stuff mentioned above. Therefore it should come as no surprise that people will believe in the God contained in the book about him.

65% of people believe that James Bond was a real person and that the first four novels about him were based on true life stories. That's an example of an unverified fact published in a book. This book. It may be a fact or it may be a complete fabrication. People often don't notice or can't tell the difference. Or simply don't care, but much later they remember it and think it might be true. I think I read it somewhere. Or did I make it up?

It's the ability of the human brain to imagine and describe the imagined thing to others, along with the associated ability to comprehend and believe abstract stuff made up by others, that caused God to be created in the human brain and also believed by the human brain, though possibly not the same human brain.

What's the weakest part of the human mind? Our memories are ridiculously unreliable, at least as far as details are concerned, but it's our capacity for self-deception that may be much more of a liability. First we invent something, then we believe it's real. Even if it turns out to be something that causes division and brutality and intolerance and war and misery.

We can only hope that evolution will eventually make our

brains less susceptible to believing bullshit and that we don't all kill each other fighting over bullshit before that happens.

The Human Personality

The human brain can be regarded from two different perspectives. It functions as a computer that can process information to control physical functions and it's a sentient organism that can understand abstract concepts and make moral decisions.

As a computer, the brain is an awesome machine with the ability to process constant streams of all manner of input data, including sights, sounds, smells, tastes and touch, whilst keeping the body breathing, pumping blood, crapping, sweating, sleeping, getting horny, pissing, controlling limbs and almost countless other physiological functions involved in keeping the human body fully functional and healthy.

Our brains may well be keeping more separate functions operating in a coordinated manner than would occur on, for example, an aircraft carrier, including all the planes taking off and landing. (That's just a guess.) But as impressive as that is, many living creatures, including capybaras, have brains capable of doing all that.

So whilst we can give a huge nod of admiration to brains for all that computational stuff, the difference between humans and other animals is that most animals are fairly predictable in their behaviour. We know which ones are likely to be dangerous. Crocodiles, always dangerous. Guinea pigs, never dangerous. (At least not lethal.) Sparrows, mostly harmless and even if they do crap on you it's a fairly minor event. Dogs… not so obvious. Tail wags and growling sounds are clues, foam dripping from a rabid mouth is a big tell.

The humans that are likely to kill us or steal from us or otherwise do us harm are nowhere near as easy to recognise. Humans are good at concealing their true nature. Which many do on account of the fact that they're malignant assholes, and they know that if everybody was aware of that, they would be treated in the manner they deserve. Many assholes join corporations or political organisations to reap the comfort of being surrounded by like-minded assholes.

Humans can be generous, caring, sharing, compassionate or the complete opposite. Most are somewhere in between. Human nature is so complex and varied that there are thousands of words that can apply. Here are just a few -

Loving, caring, smart, hard-working, lazy, relatable, gorgeous, classy, loyal, honest, hateful, crooked, dishonest, selfish, stupid. And lots more, but that's enough for now.

Human personality is like a cable TV subscription. It's only available as a package deal. Every package comes with varying amounts of malevolence, beneficence, intellectual curiosity, creativity, responsibility, sociability, compassion, intelligence, sporting ability and other stuff.

OJ Simpson got a sports package and movie star super deal but that came bundled with the jealous rage and vicious murder pack. Bill Cosby got the entertainer package along with the drug rapist option. Stephen Hawking got the super smart package but that didn't come with a fully functional body pack.

The True Story of Cappy Barra

In 2009 in an outer suburb of Houston, Texas, a middle-aged man named Malcolm "Cappy" Barra, came to the realisation that he was not happy with the cable package that he was receiving. No, that's not quite accurate. He'd never been happy with his cable package because he was paying for seven hundred and fifty-three channels he never watched along with the four channels he actually did watch. Cappy, so nicknamed at the age of four, on account of being the first person interviewed on a local TV station whilst wearing a cap backwards, had finally become sufficiently annoyed to voluntarily face the prospect of spending hours listening to unbearable elevator music played through a system that possibly used a rusty old kitchen sieve as a speaker cone.

Cappy arranged snacks and drinks on the table next to his Laz-y-Boy, emptied his bladder, and dialled. He had to listen to a menu that required him to key in the numbers 2, 3, 5 and 0, and then his customer number, which was on an invoice that he had the presence of mind to have at hand. Cappy was prepared. The cable company computer placed Cappy in the hold queue and started the hideous music. Cappy switched his phone to speaker and turned on the TV. He selected his favourite sports channel which was showing a rerun of an Olympic marathon. Not normally a distance running fan, Cappy could see the cosmic significance of watching a marathon while he waited, so he settled in. At the five-mile mark, Cappy heard the music on his phone stop. He lifted the phone to his ear but there was nothing. He said hello. Nothing on the other end. He said hello three more times before a series of beeps announced that his call had been disconnected.

Lesser men would have sworn and blasphemed at this point, but Cappy was resolute. He'd prepared for this. There were still plenty of snacks and drinks available. He went through the lengthy dialling procedure once more and set the phone down as the muzak started again. As the leader of the marathon passed the fifteen-mile mark the music stopped. Cappy picked up the phone and to his delight there was a human voice on the other end. When he described the nature of his enquiry, Cappy was told that he'd been connected to the wrong department, but the call centre person was obliging enough to redirect his call without him having to start again at the back of the first queue.

Sadly another series of beeps indicated that the transfer had not succeeded. Cappy decided to add a six-pack of beer and a bottle of Jack Daniels to his side table for the next leg of the marathon.

This time he keyed in the numbers 2, 3, 4 and 0 before keying in his customer number. At the halfway mark, twenty-one miles, Cappy's phone went directly from hold music to the disconnect beeps. Cappy opened a beer and nailed two shots of Jack, before going through the lengthy process of getting back to the sound of the most annoying music on earth.

At twenty-eight miles Cappy was once again connected to a human voice. As he tried to explain his dissatisfaction regarding the content of his cable package he was told that the records showed that he was being supplied with exactly the channels he'd selected. He tried at length to explain that there was no free choice involved in the selection of channels but the call centre operator seemed to have trouble understanding his problem, perhaps because the option packages were different in Mumbai or perhaps because people who worked in the call centre in Mumbai could not afford cable and had therefore never been exposed to the sadistic tyranny of the malevolently unattractive package deals offered by cable and other technology companies.

The operator offered Mister Barra the opportunity to change his package selection but said it would be easier for Mister Barra to do that himself on the website, for if they became disconnected while the operator was trying to make changes he might end up with a package he was not happy with. Or no package at all. Cappy took a moment to grapple with that but the phone started beeping once more and the moment was gone.

Cappy nailed another two shots of Jack and a beer as he

dialled once more, this time using options 2, 3, 3, and 0. His resolute composure was starting to slip. At the thirty-mile mark, his call for help was answered. The operator sounded sympathetic. She was about to tell him what she could do when an automated voice interrupted to tell Cappy his phone was out of credit and he would need to top up immediately or he would be disconnected. The beeps following the end of the voice recording indicated that immediately was a very accurate time estimate. Cappy reached for the Jack Daniels. Ignoring the shot glass, he guzzled a big swig straight from the bottle.

On the TV one of the marathon runners was getting the rubbery legs thing. Cappy knew how he felt. The last slug of Jack saw to that. He decided to step out for a breath of fresh air. He walked out into the front yard with a mild stagger on and turned back to face the house. His eyes went up almost magnetically to the satellite dish on the roof. He lurched to the roadside, picked up a handful of small rocks and started hurling them at the satellite dish.

"Motherfuckers!" he screamed. "You pack of fucking shitbag motherfuckers!" The rocks mostly missed the dish but one of them hit it and bounced off, smashing the window of the house next door. Cappy didn't seem to notice. He kept hurling the rocks.

The front door of the neighbouring house opened. Max Stirrup stepped out onto his porch. He was holding an AR-15 rifle with a high-capacity magazine, his trigger finger rigid alongside the trigger guard, indicating proudly to all lesser men that he knew his way around a gun. "What the fuck are you doing, Cappy? Stop that shit right now!"

Cappy glared at him. "Or what? Or fucking what? You going to shoot me, Stirrup? You gonna fuckin' shoot me?" Cappy marched threateningly towards him. Stirrup hadn't seen Cappy like this before. Ever. They'd been neighbours for fifteen years and Cappy had always been a quiet, peaceful guy. Now he looked like a maniac.

"Take it easy, Cappy. No one's gonna shoot no one."

"So what's with the fuckin' gun?"

"I didn't know it was you. Someone smashed my fuckin' window. What am I meant to think?"

Cappy walked right up to him. The gun was pointed down at the ground. They locked eyes. Cappy lunged for the gun. Stirrup did not expect that. In a flash it was the angry Cappy who was now the one with the deadly weapon.

"What the fuck, Cappy? What's going on?"

Cappy stumbled back over to his own yard. He aimed the gun at his own satellite dish and fired. Stirrup ducked back inside. Although most of the bullets missed, enough hit the dish to ensure its destruction.

"Yee ha, take that, motherfuckers." Cappy walked into the road. He stopped at each house, blowing away every satellite dish and TV aerial that he saw. The marathon re-run was nearing its end although Cappy had forgotten all about that. So absorbed was he in his suburban shooting gallery that he was also seemingly oblivious to the sound of approaching police sirens. His phone rang in his pocket. Cappy was surprised. He answered it.

"Hello, we got cut off. I was trying to organise a new cable package for you." That was the last thing Cappy ever heard. He didn't hear the bullet that ripped the phone from his hand, or the one that went through his head, or the fifteen other police bullets that tore through his body, or the twenty-three bullets that missed including the bullet that killed a tiger that had wandered into the street a block behind Cappy.

At his funeral, one of the eulogists told the story of how Cappy got his nickname. A tiger had escaped from the yard of an eccentric individual in Rosenberg, Texas, and had been roaming the district for three days. Cappy's family lived a few doors along from the tiger's owner where a TV crew from a local station saw four-year-old Cappy riding his trike, and not having found anything vaguely newsworthy, the local news reporter decided to interview him. As the reporter was asking him why he wore his cap backwards, the camera quickly panned away to frame the escaped tiger as it walked into the street, just four or five houses away, where it was immediately shot by a local resident with an AR-15.

The second appearance of a tiger at a big moment in Cappy's life drew a variety of opinions from those at his wake. They ranged from "wild coincidence", to "major cosmic spiritual sign from God", to "What if someone just made it up? Has anyone seen the footage? No. Does the footage still exist? Unlikely. It was forty years ago. So the whole thing could just be bullshit right?"

Cappy not only had the wrong cable package installed, he had the wrong emotional packages installed in his brain. His anger suppression package was good, but ultimately not good enough, and his anger venting package, whilst having a much higher than usual threshold, was a liability. Despite Cappy's unwillingness to directly harm or kill people, his personality trait packages became a hazard for those around him. Especially tigers.

The number and variety of human personality traits is huge. The range of personality trait packages is almost infinitely large. And that needs to be considered when evaluating the excellence or otherwise of the human brain as the creation of God.

Personality traits can be categorised as good, bad and ugly, and are also, unfortunately, supplied in bundles that contain traits from different categories giving rise to the complex issue that most people are neither completely good nor completely bad, although there have always been complete assholes who have so much bad and ugly in them that they can be scientifically classified as evil shit stains on humanity.

Obviously I'm not the first human to notice that there are types or archetypes of personality and types of personality traits, but like everything from trying to organise a computer filing system to tidying up the garage, putting things into accurately categorised boxes is never as simple as it appears to be at the outset. If Carl Jung had been exposed to cable TV packs I feel fairly certain he would have gone for a similar analogy, although he would have almost certainly expanded on the simple cable TV analogy by including bundles, as in Broadband with a Streaming Sport and Horror pack and a home phone line with 120 free minutes.

Things the Professionals Say

Most psychology professionals do not use the service-provider-industry-standard-treadmill-of-never-ending-payments-bundle analogy when describing the human brain. Probably because they have a desire to be taken seriously. They do however invent categories and sub-categories and try to shove everything into the resulting boxes. With varying levels of success.

The Big Five Personality Traits

Getting broad acceptance of something like the categories of personality traits is like crossing a minefield of professional jealousy and disagreement brought about by the composition and influence of the various personality traits of those trying to do the categorising. Miraculously, after about 30 years of bitter backstabbing, name-calling and slander, a number, five, was agreed on in 1961. Ernest Tupes and Raymond Christal were credited with identifying the five personality traits that were immediately and repeatedly re-analysed and renamed by many others. Arguably the big winner, after another twenty years of the big-time mud wrestling that is professional psychology, was Lewis Goldberg who prevailed in 1981 in the fight for the credit for overall naming rights with the elegant and simple, yet powerful moniker, The Big Five.

Colleagues of Goldberg claimed that he had enlisted the

help of his brother-in-law, a well-known, though not well-respected Madison Avenue advertising executive, called Louis Pultza. Pultza had a reputation for stealing concepts, so the true genius behind the naming of The Big Five will probably never be known.

The Big Five Personality Traits are -

Openness to experience, intellectual curiosity and creativity

Conscientiousness, productivity, responsibility

Extroversion, sociability, assertiveness

Agreeableness, empathy, respectfulness, trust

Neuroticism, anxiety, depression

And then along came HEXACO.

In a science as inexact as psychology, nothing will ever truly be settled, and naturally some smarty pants would eventually come up with a number larger than five. Unsurprisingly that number was six.

The Six-Factor Model of Personality bounded into the ring in the early 2000s with a name befitting a scientific breakthrough for the twenty-first century - HEXACO. All caps, all the time. HEXACO. Fuck you I'm HEXACO. Whether it really was a 21st-century breakthrough or just some more shit someone made up, is open to debate, and given the field we're looking at it would be a fair bet to say that some deep thinkers are probably arguing the merits of five, six, or perhaps even seven or eight traits, right at this moment.

HEXACO is basically the big five (with some modifications and redefinitions, obviously) with the addition of number six, honesty-humility. That's "honesty-humility" with a hyphen. Like the father of Major Major Major in Catch-22, the inventors of HEXACO (all caps, fuck you) were not about to let the naming of a brand new trait, a major new trait, number goddam six if you fucking well please, go by without inventing a new word and a compound one at that. Why use two existing words when you can claim that you invented a new one by inserting a hyphen?

If that's not enough jargon, you could visit the HEXACO-PI-R website which "contains basic information and materials for the HEXACO Personality Inventory-Revised, an instrument that assesses the six major dimensions of personality:"

- Honesty-Humility

- Emotionality

- eXtraversion

- Agreeableness (versus Anger)

- Conscientiousness

- Openness to Experience

The team behind HEXACO not only revised and re-ordered the earlier five traits, but elevated their new one to number one. That's number ONE. All caps. HEXACO. Fuck you.

By the time Goldberg and Pultza noticed that they could have named The Big Five, "OCEAN - The Big Five", or "The Big Five OCEAN", or even "OCEAN's Five", the HEXACO brigade had rearranged the order of traits and it was too late baby.

The Dark Core of Personality   aka the D-factor

This book is not concerned with the human brain according to psychologists, it's a look at the human brain as the deliberate, intelligent design of God. So we're mostly interested in personality traits of the biblical kind. The ones concerning good and evil. The traits responsible for humans being good bastards or bad bastards.

Psychologists have, unsurprisingly, had a bit of a think about the not-so-nice aspects of human nature and so came up with the Dark Core of Personality also known as The Dark Triad and then, oh so predictably, the Dark Tetrad.

The Dark Triad was an invention of researchers Paulhus and Williams in 2002. They decided that a dash of narcissism mixed in with a bit of psychopathy and a sprinkle of Machiavellianism was all a human needed to indulge in truly evil behaviours. Hard to argue with that. One of those traits makes a person difficult if not impossible to share a house with. Two of them and you have an unbearable neighbour. All three and you have a thoroughly rotten dictator.

As if anything could add to the general nastiness of the above three traits, The Dark Tetrad one-ups the Dark Triad by adding sadism to the mix. It's easy to assume that all psychopaths are sadists, as that's how they are often portrayed in movies, but there is a difference between being indifferent to suffering and enjoying it to the degree that you will take steps to cause suffering and torture people purely for your own entertainment.

A malignant narcissist is bad enough, but one who is also a sadist? Look out! Triad, fuck you. I'm TETRAD. DARK TETRAD. All caps, fuck you. And I'm a bad muthafucka.

Narcissists - Require praise, admiration and adulation. Can't tolerate criticism.

Psychopaths - Lack empathy and are therefore callous and ruthless. Do not care about the wishes of others.

Machiavellians - Will do anything to achieve their goals. Anything.

Sadists - Derive pleasure from the pain of others.

There is often a large measure of overlap of the above traits in bad bastards, and the Tetrad is pretty much an ascending scale of bastardry.

The God of the Old Testament clearly ticked the first three boxes with respect to his first four commandments and his smiting and drowning and hellfire, but whether he was also a sadist is arguable, though highly likely, given that you might not bother to set up a perpetual torture dungeon unless you got some pleasure from it.

The D-factor vs the g factor (general intelligence)

An important thing to notice about the traits of the DARK TETRAD is that they are independent of intelligence. In other words, you are just as likely to get a dumb as a mud fence, murderous thug as you are to get a genius Professor Evil working on a machine to facilitate mass torture. Professor Evil is, of course, a much bigger problem than a random stupid thug. Except for those in the immediate vicinity or presence of the stupid, murderous thug.

A really disturbing thing, that's possibly the key to why the world is so fucked up, is that the first three dark traits are almost a recipe for success in a competitive world.

A narcissist will be highly motivated to succeed in order to get the praise and adulation that he requires. A non-narcissist, not so much.

A psychopath will make sure he gets what he wants regardless of the effect on others. An empathetic person will consider the impact on others and try not to harm them.

A Machiavellian will not hesitate to lie and cheat his way to the top. A decent man will be held in check by his principles.

All of which is helpful in understanding why so many of these arseholes end up in charge of everything, from school committees to town councils to corporations to countries.

Perhaps a bright future for humanity would require the development of a test for the DARK TETRAD traits. Any person wishing to run for public office would be tested and those exhibiting high levels of dark tendencies would be excluded from elections. Unfortunately, it would be difficult to devise such a test and even if it were possible, the bad bastards in charge would never allow it to be implemented. Because bad bastards love power, and they do not relinquish it.

Nice guys aren't prepared to get down and dirty and lie and cheat and so they finish last. Sad but true. It only takes one bad bastard to beat a whole field of nice guys.

Looking at the human brain as the creation of God it seems fair to say that God did an appalling job of allocating personality traits. Programming human brains in such a way that evil has a head start is not very nice, to say the least.

But then again, if God created man in his own image, then he did a very good job as the traits of the Dark Core of Personality could serve as an accurate depiction of the character of the God of the Old Testament.

We're Good, We're Bad, We're Average, We're Ugly

Ugly people flick cigarette butts out of car windows kinda hoping to ignite the tinder-dry tussock they're driving past.

Bad people throw fast food debris out car windows because they just don't give a shit. And because they're stupid.

Average people don't throw trash out of car windows.

Good people stop and pick up the trash thrown out by the bad people. And they put out the fires of the ugly. Make that very good people. Very good people with martyr-ish tendencies and no need to get where they're going in a timely manner.

These categories are fairly arbitrary, and they pretty much have to be. We're not simple. Most of us have the capacity to do good things and bad things, so there's a lot of overlap in the following sections.

THE GOOD

The Nice Bits

Intelligence

Intelligence is the first topic in this section because it's the most amazing thing about the human brain.

Intelligent people are responsible for the advancement of humanity. Unintelligent people, whatever else they may contribute to the workforce and civilisation in general, don't contribute much to the advancement of anything. In some cases, they can be more like a handbrake on progress. Often because of their beliefs.

How many people born today would discover the principle of flight had it not already been discovered? Not many. Lots of us live in high-rise buildings, but how many would be able to figure out how to build the one they live in? Or even a low-rise? Complete with power and plumbing and all the other technology that makes it work as a comfortable dwelling? Not many, if any. What proportion of people could design and construct an engine of any kind? It's that small proportion of humanity with a high level of intelligence that we all lean on, all day, every day without even being aware of it.

Intelligence is the most brilliant thing about the human brain. It's the thing that allows us to think and talk about stuff like this.

If the whole human race was of average intelligence it's doubtful that we would have invented the wheel yet. A fairly

NOT VERY INTELLIGENT DESIGN THREE

testy debate recently popped up in New Zealand about something called Matauranga Maori, the Maori "way of knowing", also referred to as "Maori science". It's a topic that involves a lot more than we're dealing with here, so we'll stick to a very simple view. Given that there's no such thing as French Science or Italian Science, I can't think of any good reason to establish a branch of science defined by a racial grouping. Science is science. That's a full stop there. It doesn't matter who discovers something first, because if that person didn't discover it, someone else would have done so, some time later.

If humans suddenly lost all knowledge of everything, but we retained our intelligence, it's a certainty that eventually all of our scientific knowledge would be rediscovered. Because it will still be there, waiting to be discovered. It's also a certainty that there would be many religions, although none of the current ones, because they're not based on anything that can be rediscovered. They need to be invented. Out of whole cloth, as Christopher Hitchens was fond of saying. Along with all art and fiction, existing religions would be lost forever. But I digress.

It's a fact that by the time of the arrival of Europeans (about 350 years or so after the arrival of the Maori), Maori had not invented the wheel, or any form of metal, but describing Maori as Stone Age people is regarded as a racist slur. Which it most certainly is. Because the only people who say it are racists being deliberately racist.

The Proud Boys organisation describes itself as a collection of "Western chauvinists who refuse to apologise for creating the modern world". Oh, really? How were they involved in creating the modern world? What exactly did they contribute to make them think they could claim the credit for the brilliant achievements of individuals to whom they are not even remotely related? Has any one of those Dunning-Kruger-afflicted morons ever invented anything more useful than a punch in the face?

The reason for this particular rant is this -

If a few hundred people of European descent arrived in New Zealand under the same conditions (meaning none of them had ever seen a wheel, or anything made of metal) as when the Maori arrived, would they have fared any better in that three hundred and fifty years? Would they have invented the wheel? Figured out how to make bronze, or iron, or glass?

Not a chance. No way. Not unless there was a one-in-a-billion genius amongst them. And even then probably not. As demonstrated by Jared Diamond, for anybody to have the luxury of enough time to think about inventing or building anything new, there had to be enough food available to feed them along with the willingness of those who participated in gathering that food, to share it. New Zealand was not naturally endowed with nutritious crops that were easy to grow and store, or animals that were able to be farmed, so nobody back then had much time to do anything except go out hunting and gathering. Although they did manage to build quite impressively fortified villages.

New Zealand had no native pigs or goats or sheep or cattle. In fact, the only land mammals native to New Zealand were two species of bat. They are reportedly delicious, but like quail or baby chipmunks you have to eat quite a few of them if you've worked up an appetite that's gonna take some beddin' down.

The bronze and iron ages began in the fertile crescent of the Middle East, so named because of the abundance of naturally occurring, labour-saving farm animals and crops. They had more time to build things and invent things than people living elsewhere. Yet it still took the combined efforts of the smartest people in the fertile places thousands of years to invent bronze, iron and glass. Singling out a small, isolated population for not keeping pace with the rest of the planet is really stupid. Many white men (not just proud boys) are happy to bask in the glory of their gifted ancestors as if they could have invented all the useful stuff if it hadn't already been invented. But they're deluding themselves.

Economist Milton Friedman used the making of a pencil as an introduction to talk about other things that we're not dealing with here. He pointed out that hardly any individual would be able to describe every step necessary to make a pencil from raw materials, and almost nobody, probably exactly nobody, would succeed if they tried to make one without the help of others. Could you accurately name all the raw materials required? I couldn't. I couldn't even name the raw materials in the paint on the pencil. Let alone how to make the lead. Or the metal bit holding the rubber on. Or the rubber.

If you took ten million people from modern-day USA, screened them to ensure that nobody was of above average intelligence and put them on a sufficiently large island with enough natural resources to survive, but nothing other than the clothes they were wearing, what would you find when you returned a hundred years later? Would you find a thriving, well-governed, technology-driven civilisation with power, plumbing, trading and transport systems? Or would you find hundreds, or thousands, of tribes living in a constant state of primitive warfare? Would they have all died from disease and malnutrition?

It's hard to say. There'd have been some among them who would have known how to rebuild a transmission, but could they have made one from scratch? No. So their knowledge of transmissions would have been lost, unless someone figured out how to preserve it. Which would be unlikely, because the immediate needs would have been shelter and food, not paper and pencil. Without a few smart people to invent, create and execute good ideas, the prognosis would be poor. The only thing we can be certain of is that they would have created a few gods to fight over, and there'd be some with the cult leader gene who'd make up some terrible rules and have sex with a lot of children.

It took two or three hundred thousand years for all of the combined intellect of humanity to begin to invent anything. But once we got started... it still took a while. From the invention of the wheel to the first motor car took about three to three and a half thousand years. In that time, meaning the last few years of that time, a whole lot of things started being invented and things really took off. Twenty years after the first motor car sputtered to life came the first powered flight. Just sixty years after that people were drinking champagne whilst flying on Pan Am Clipper Jets between New York and London and the first man stood on the moon. Magnificent.

Human intelligence is an incredible thing, but the thing that's way more incredible is the ability of humans to communicate, store and utilise ideas that build our communal intelligence into a body of knowledge that increases exponentially to create the world we live in.

And not only the world we live in but the bodies we live in. Bodies that are much healthier, much more disease resistant, bodies that last longer and look and smell better than ever before.

Sometimes, with the help of David Attenborough, we marvel at the way ants can build a giant anthill. Or an ant bridge. But compared to Manhattan? How about the fact that around half a million people are flying in aeroplanes, miles above the ground, at any given moment? That's some seriously powerful communal intelligence.

Unfortunately, the inventions of intelligent people are now providing those with below-average intelligence a much louder voice than they've ever had before, which is to the benefit of nobody, least of all themselves. Where this situation may lead is the subject of the movie Idiocracy, which is both amusing and terrifying (and well worth a watch), especially as it's much closer to the reality of 2023 than when it was made in 2006.

If there was a rule that people were only allowed to express opinions using equipment that they could give a very rudimentary explanation of how it worked, we could be spared the strident cries of morons tweeting about everything from gun control to abortion to deep state 5G vaccination murders. (I'm not trying to imply that I think I'm anywhere near smart enough to have invented any of the technology that's advanced human civilisation, but at least I can understand how some of it works when it's explained to me.)

To have an opinion published on the letters to the editor page of a newspaper in days gone by, the writer had to demonstrate at least a rudimentary grasp of the subject at hand as well as some competence in grammar, punctuation and spelling. Today there's no barrier to impede illiterate fools from flooding Twitter with their often incomprehensible brain farts. As Dunning and Kruger pointed out, they have no idea how little they know. About anything. (I'm temporarily ignoring the role played by exponents of misinformation in manipulating the gullible to amplify their malevolent agenda, but we'll get to that in a later section.)

Every time a reporter with a camera and a microphone tests the general knowledge of people in the street, the results are horrifying. "What was the name of the first human to walk on the sun?" "Um ah er Armstrong? Lance Armstrong?" "I said the sun, not the moon." "Oh, right… aaah… Matt Damon?"

Democracy relies on the votes of the people. It also relies on those people not being idiots. But it does nothing to ensure that that's the case. Traditionally most idiots couldn't be bothered voting, but in this new age of the rise of the militant moron, perhaps there needs to be some kind of filter to ensure that the votes of the not-so-bright don't count. Perhaps by means of a voting competency test on every ballot paper.

For example, a multi-guess quiz that should be pretty easy for anybody who thinks their opinion, in the form of a vote, should be taken seriously -

US Federal Ballot Paper Page 1

1.   How many Senators are there in the United States Senate?
a   52
b   256
c   100
d   200

2. How many US states have no land boundary?
    In other words, how many US States are entirely
    surrounded by water?
a   One
b   Two
c   Three
d   None

3. Which of the following is a country in Europe?
    (Pick one, even though there may be more than one correct
    answer).
a   Africa
b   France
c   Asia
d   Italy

4. What are the three branches of the US Government?
a   Judicial, Ecclesiastical, Local
b   Executive, Management, Systematic
c   Legislative, Executive, Judicial
d   Judicial, Contemplative, Executive

5. According to the US Constitution, which branch of the US
    government must take into account the word of God
    according to the Bible?
a   Legislative
b   Judicial
c   Executive
d   None of the above

All voting papers with 3 or more correct answers will be counted in
the ballot.

Contrast the stupidity and arrogance of the Proud Boys
("Western chauvinists who refuse to apologise for creating

the modern world"), with the awareness and humility of a truly intelligent human being.

> From: Steve Jobs
>
> To: Steve Jobs
>
> Date: Thursday, September 2, 2010 at 11:08 PM
>
> I grow little of the food I eat, and of the little I do grow I did not breed or perfect the seeds.
>
> I do not make any of my own clothing.
>
> I speak a language I did not invent or refine.
>
> I did not discover the mathematics I use.
>
> I am protected by freedoms and laws I did not conceive of or legislate, and do not enforce or adjudicate.
>
> I am moved by music I did not create myself.
>
> When I needed medical attention, I was helpless to help myself survive.
>
> I did not invent the transistor, the microprocessor, object oriented programming, or most of the technology I work with.
>
> I love and admire my species, living and dead, and am totally dependent on them for my life and well being.
>
> Sent from my iPad

If the human brain evolved, then the intelligence of the smartest among us is seriously impressive, and the variation in the intelligence of the rest is exactly what we'd expect from an evolutionary process.

If God created the human brain, then well done to the big lad. For the intelligent ones that is. It's just a shame that he didn't make most of us quite a lot brighter.

And why so many with the attributes of the DARK TETRAD? A truly intelligent designer, one with a hint of benevolence at least, would have made sure that there were a lot fewer of those bastards to inflict brutal dictatorship conditions on the rest of us, whether at a national, state, workplace, educational or household level.

Muscle memory

As well as the philosophical and behavioural aspects of the human brain we should also have a quick look at the physical control function.

We all know that muscles themselves don't learn anything, even though it feels like they do. We do thousands of things every day that require our muscles to move in complex ways, yet we do them without giving our muscles any conscious thought. Only when a task is new or fiddly, do we need to concentrate on the actions of our limbs and digits, but even then we do so at a level removed from the muscles themselves. We can't even tell which muscles we're using most of the time. Try lifting an arm and waving, then clapping hands. Could you identify the individual muscles you just used? That doesn't mean naming them, just feeling them.

So it's not surprising that we credit our muscles with remembering what to do even though we understand that every intricate electrical impulse that activated those muscles came from our brains. Perhaps muscle memory should be called something more like auto-muscle pilot or full self motion.

When Jackie Chan first dazzled movie audiences with his slapstick gymnastic excellence, he was breaking new ground. These days there are thousands of people with Red Bull logos on their outfits or equipment performing unbelievable physical feats that just a few years ago would have been widely regarded as impossible.

They jump off mountains wearing wing suits and fly themselves into the open door of a passing aeroplane. They ride mountain bikes down the most impossible tracks either on mountainsides or through favelas. They fly parachute wings through alpine villages bouncing their skis off walls and rooftops as they go. All of these things are amazing. Unlike climbing mountains or deep diving and holding your breath to the point where your blood boils, which are just stupid.

When some French street thieves started demonstrating their ability to run up and across walls and jump from rooftops landing in an armadillo roll (not to be confused with a delicious Bolivian sushi), it seemed like we had pushed the human body to the limit and further amazing feats would become rarer. Not yet, apparently. Even gymnasts, performing within tight rules and guidelines that have existed for a long time, continue to amaze us with astonishing new moves. The tricks now routinely performed by world-class skiers, snowboarders and skateboarders are barely believable.

Even though other animals on planet Earth have certain superior physical attributes to humans, none of them have made the significant advances that we have. The fastest cheetah on earth today would be about the same speed as the fastest cheetah of two hundred years ago. A few nights before writing this, I watched the Highlanders (a professional rugby team from Dunedin, NZ) destroy the Waratahs (an Australian team) by 59 points to 23. One of the people watching with me suggested that even the losing team in this humiliation would have beaten the best rugby team on the planet of thirty years earlier (almost certainly the All Blacks) and by a much bigger margin. There was no disagreement. The worst player on the field in the modern game would be significantly better than the best player in the world thirty years ago. The levels of skill and fitness have increased massively as have the tactics and strategies.

Once again, even in physical pursuits, the difference between humans and animals comes down to our ability for the best to pass on their knowledge to the rest and so dramatically improve the performance of humankind overall. What improvements are still possible remains to be seen.

When the human brain is functioning well, it's amazing. The ability of the human brain to take the raw input of light in the eyeballs and transpose that into a real-world, 3D-picture that makes perfect sense to us as it constantly changes is nothing short of incredible. That it also instantly combines that input with inputs from the other senses, sound, touch, taste, and smell and analyses it all with regard to the accumulated knowledge in our memory is even more incredible. The computing power involved is staggering to think about it.

We sometimes get a glimpse of the process in those moments when we're looking at something in low light or a part of a small image, perhaps on a screen, that we have yet to comprehend. It can take a moment for the group of colours to make sense. Sometimes we see the wrong thing first. Often a face. But when the actual thing comes into focus, or more accurately into comprehension, we suddenly see it for what it really is. When our brain takes a tenth of a millisecond to understand that it's highly unlikely that we're looking at a crouching tiger or hidden dragon, it correctly re-identifies the object as a garbage bag. Which we then see clearly.

Usually our brains interpret these electrical impulses so quickly and accurately that we're entirely unaware of it. But our brains are doing this with incredible accuracy every waking moment of our lives. In the background. At the same time we're thinking about what we'd like for lunch, wow she's pretty, what time was I meeting him, mustn't forget to buy the wine, and five other simultaneous thoughts, whilst driving in three lanes of traffic listening to a podcast about the Titanic.

Tesla is getting closer to having the cameras and computers on cars do a similar job, but even when they perfect the thing, it will be nowhere near the ability of the human brain. It won't see a cat in the driveway and think, "There's my darling little fluffy friend", or "Where did that cat come from, I've not seen that one before", or "There's that bloody neighbour's cat I'll bet it's been shitting in my rose garden again". It will merely think, "Small animate object, try not to squish it, but not in such an extreme manner that you'll harm your occupants". As you can probably tell, I have no idea how the AI in a Tesla will think about these things but it's fair to say it will be nothing like the way we do because its task is different. It has no need to feel emotion or make complex connections when it sees Fluffy.

As amazing as the human brain is at computing all our senses into a complete image of the reality around us it's not a complete reality. It's just a version of reality as we understand it. There are colours we don't see and sounds we don't hear, and if we could receive and comprehend all the information in the electromagnetic waves all around us we would be bombarded with a thousand radio and television signals simultaneously. Real reality, total reality, would be unbearable. In other words, our senses are geared to function on a need-to-know basis.

Yet as wonderful and amazing as all that is, there's nothing unique about the human brain in being able to do that comprehension and computation thing. There are thousands of species of sentient creatures on the planet who do much the same thing in terms of understanding the world in which they live. In most regards the human brain functions in the same way as many other species. In other regards we're way better.

We can ride a bicycle better than a capybara without ever considering the need to maintain balance. Our brains just do it automatically. The human brain can learn to play a musical instrument with such speed and precision and emotion that fingers move with agility and finesse far beyond the conscious level. Some human brains can look at a piece of music in its written form, a piece of music which in its essence is mathematical, and transform it, in performance, to a level of beauty and emotion that can feel almost spiritual.

Good work brains. Amazing.

Wisdom, kindness and empathy

In addition to intelligence, many traits of the human brain are really good, including kindness, philanthropy, empathy, cooperation, decency, organisation, creativity, work ethic etc. The good attributes of the human brain, as demonstrated by the behaviour of human beings with well-functioning brains, can be put into two categories.

The first category of good humans is those who do no harm. Or at least try to do no harm. As found in the Golden Rule. The one rule to rule them all. Treat others the way you'd like others to treat you. Be fair. Be polite. Be kind. Be honest. Be respectful. Be decent. Try really hard not to be a dick.

Humans that live by the golden rule are fine people. If everybody lived by that one simple code the world would be a much easier place to live. Although possibly a little dull as there'd be no baddies and therefore no crime dramas to binge on Netflix or anywhere else. Would there be enough of a struggle to make existence interesting in a world devoid of bad people? Yeah, I think so. When it comes to the sort of gun-slinging baddies that we like to watch on screens, most people I know never come across them in real life. Unless they go to school, or church, or concerts, or shopping malls in America that is. In other western countries we come across common thieves and fraudsters often enough. We just have to go to the bank or have a phone or the internet or do a bit of shopping for that to happen, but we're so used to being ripped off by "legitimate" businesses that it mostly doesn't bother us too much. And yet even for relatively wealthy Westerners, life is still somewhat of a struggle and not, for most of us, so easy as to be boring.

We have enough knowledge and technology right now to make the lives of everybody on earth fairly comfortable if only there weren't so many amoral, greedy bastards, and so many idiots who think tribalism and its inherent, never-ending conflict is a good idea. It's a bit of a dilemma really. The concept of a world inhabited only by decent people may be a topic for an interesting hypothetical discussion but it would be of little value because the chance of anything like that ever coming about, given human nature, is zero.

We've got pretty good at dealing with problems that are not of our own making. Even if the shit really hits the fan such as when a hurricane, tsunami, volcanic eruption or pandemic strikes, we're often reasonably good at dealing with it and getting things back to normal in a fairly timely manner. It's what decent humans do. Unless human stupidity or corruption steps in to make things worse such as during the Covid-19 pandemic, or some hurricane responses. Declaring that God sent the hurricane because of all the gay bars in the area is as useful as sending thoughts and prayers, but with added malevolent bigotry.

The Golden Rule doesn't work in all circumstances. Masochists would need a special interpretation document, though there'd be no need for a version for sociopaths and sadists, because they're not going to even try to co-operate. Neither are those who enjoy fighting in public bars and football stadiums, or on trains travelling to and from football stadiums. The Golden Rule is also not usually followed by those who belong to a tribe that believes they deserve different treatment from other tribes, usually because their leaders have told them their god said they're the special ones, and so they're allowed to treat others with contempt and sometimes even kill them by throwing rocks at their heads.

The second category of good humans, arguably the top level of humanity, are those that do significantly more good than harm. They not only don't throw trash, they pick it up. They not only don't kick a homeless person, they help him. These are wonderful people, though very rare. They appear on the far end of the bell curve of human decency from those who think selfishness is a virtue.

There might even be two layers here. Those that do good when it's not difficult. And those that do good even when it costs them a lot, possibly financially, possibly in terms of their own safety.

Mother Teresa was often put into the selfless do-gooder category but Christopher Hitchens had plenty to say about her and her decisions that resulted in the greatly increased suffering of those in her care. Apparently her motivation was a belief in bible verses that said suffering brought one closer to God. Either that or she was just an evil sadist.

Empathy is probably the most important trait of a decent person. It can easily be argued that all that is required for evil to prevail is a lack of empathy. Religions often discourage empathy by dividing people into us, the self-selected chosen ones, and them, those who are worthy of eternal damnation.

Evangelical Christian Oprah Winfrey said that atheists can't feel awe and wonder. Without meaning to (we'll give her the benefit of the doubt) she revealed her contempt for those who are not of her tribe, and her feeling that others were fundamentally inferior.

A wise person would refrain from making sweeping generalisations about how other types of people think, and what other people perceive, as none of us know such things.

I'm sure Oprah has felt the sting of racial prejudice many times, especially earlier in her life, which makes her lack of understanding in this instance even less understandable. But that's what religion does to people, even mostly decent, philanthropic people like Oprah.

If the human brain is the creation of God, then he did good work on creating all the decent, moral ones. The problem is that they seem to be a small minority. On the upside, the really bad ones, the evil ones, the malignant, narcissistic psychopaths, also seem to be a small minority.

Which leaves most of us under the big bell in the middle somewhere.

A Person of Good Character

Many of the good things about the human brain can be distilled in the phrase, a person of good character. Being of good character has a few indicators. It means, for example, that there's no way you'd shag your best friend's girlfriend or boyfriend unless it was absolutely not pre-meditated, you were both really drunk and thoughts of consequences had long ago left the building. Consequences that may include no longer being considered a person of good character. Depending on who finds out.

A person is defined by their character. They may have a public persona that is far removed from their real character, but their real character is who they really are. There's a chance that many people don't know their own true character. We don't know how brave we'd be in certain situations until the moment we're tested. We don't know how much of our behaviour is guided by the expectations of others, or what we think others may think of us, whether close acquaintances or society at large.

When it was not okay to be gay, which, disgracefully, it's still not in a lot of places, gay men lived their lives pretending to be heterosexual. Many lived their whole lives hiding this part of their true selves from everybody, including their wives and children. This used to be fairly commonplace amongst politicians and still is, in some places, depending on party affiliation.

According to Plato, there are four cardinal virtues.

Wisdom. Courage. Moderation. Justice.

"Wisdom is the leader: next follows moderation; and from the union of these two with courage springs justice." ~ Plato

So wisdom and moderation together have a threesome with courage. Resulting in a moderate amount of wisdom and courage. Meaning someone of average intelligence who's not a coward. Resulting in the baby justice. Really?

Wouldn't wisdom without moderation be better? Though moderated courage might be beneficial, if it was tempered by wisdom, rather than mere moderation. Keep your head down, don't go over the top when you can see a sheet of tracer rounds whistling over the trench.

Decency, equality or fairness is not specifically mentioned by Plato here, although they would seem to have more to do with justice than moderation or courage. Wisdom should lead to justice, but is it not possible to be wise in many things, yet also be a psychopathic narcissist? In which case your idea of justice would be whatever benefits you, even if that involves the suffering of others.

An attitude or belief that's fairly widespread in humans is to hold the wisdom of our ancestors in high regard. Why is that? We don't continue to use their technology out of respect (do outside toilets, steam engines and open sewers deserve high regard?) and their ideas about colonisation, slavery, women's rights and the like are falling into disrepute at varying rates depending on the ancient beliefs of those in any given government. Legal scholars and justices spend endless hours combing through laws and precedents established when slavery was commonplace and witches were burned at the stake. Why? Why not administer law based on the more enlightened standards of today?

We're told to respect religions because they're old and established yet anyone can openly dump on cults, even though there's absolutely no difference. Just people making shit up and selling it to the gullible.

Why don't we treat ancient wisdom as we treat ancient science? Respect and a tip of the hat to the first to discover things, but we've moved on, and now we know more. A lot more. Wisdom that still stands up on its own merits, however, like an early scientific discovery that still stands, deserves ongoing respect. Respect for what it is, not respect for being old.

With regard to science, we now know more. With regard to morals, we now know better. Well, some of us do. Many human societies are still fairly barbaric, but the progress towards decency and human rights for all is nevertheless ongoing, albeit far more slowly than it should be, and that lack of progress is often the fault of an established religion. Which must be respected. Because of tradition and stuff. Christ we can be idiots.

If God designed the human brain, it seems he deliberately made us slow learners with respect to morals and the imperative to treat others with decency. I guess he did that because of the "in his own image" clause. He was a ruthless unforgiving bastard and he made us the same, giving us the task of becoming decent on our own.

But if the human brain evolved, then we're evolving in the right direction, and the evolution of our moral code is proceeding much faster than any physical evolution. Not as fast as the advancement of science and technology, which has the most intelligent humans contributing to it, but still faster than the advancement of decent, equal societies, perhaps because all sorts of fools, villains and charlatans can influence laws and social mores, provided they can gather enough like-minded idiots to support them.

While we can praise the best aspects of human behaviour, such as empathy, affection, love, and helping those in trouble, those traits are also often seen in non-human animals. The traits of the dark triad are somewhat rarer in the wild though it's obvious that all crocodiles and alligators are psychopaths. Some hippos too.

Sex 'n' drugs 'n' rock 'n' roll ('n' love)

Sex 'n' drugs 'n' rock 'n' roll are the big three, the trifecta of human entertainment. They're popular because they can be enjoyed individually, or together, or as a threesome, or as a threesome with drugs and music.

They're especially popular with younger adults, even to the point of being more popular than money, because when you're getting plenty of sex and drugs and rock 'n' roll, you really don't care too much for money. Cos money can't buy you love. Although it can buy you sex. However if you do get some money, drugs and rock 'n' roll is sometimes a wise investment as it increases the chances of the sex being free.

Sex

In itself, having sex is great. It's often referred to as the most fun you can have without laughing and things other than sex have been called the most fun you can have with your clothes on.

Alas, the brain complicates sexual desire to the point that it dominates, confuses and even ruins, many lives. And I'm not just talking about self-proclaimed sex addicts. What a bunch of self-obsessed wankers. We're all sex addicts for fuck's sake. Sex has the same effect on the human brain as tobacco and booze. If you haven't had a fix for a while it starts to take over your thoughts until you find merciful release. What makes sex the more powerful addiction is that it does not require any gateway mechanism. We're all randy. It's hard-wired. (Except for a tiny minority, poor bastards, but there are always exceptions.)

There are theories among the religiously minded that if you can scare children enough to make them refrain from playing with themselves, they won't develop sexual cravings. Ha ha ha ha ha ha ha ha. If you don't start smoking you won't get addicted. True. If you don't start drinking you won't get addicted. True. If you don't start wanking... get outta here... everybody starts wanking. And continues to wank. It's biology. At what age it ceases I have yet to discover. Celibacy is as big a lie as a talking snake. The only snake that talks is the one that tells you it could do with a massage.

A big part of the reason that sex is problematic for a lot of people is the brainwashing of children. Usually for religious reasons. Sometimes the "sex is dirty" mantra is societal rather than strictly religious, but a search for the origin would invariably trace back to religion. I'm not suggesting that the world would be a better place if we all just went at it like bunnies or bonobos, but the combination of "sex is dirty" and "don't be a slut" with the importance of being good at it, being "a good lay", is pretty much a recipe for potential mental issues.

Although sex is primarily a physical thing, it's also a brain thing. Whether that should be blamed on the designer of the brain rather than the operators of evolved brains is too circular to bother with. And it might make my brain hurt.

Recently I read something along the lines of - God only put enough blood in the body of a man for one head at a time - which is funny because it's true. When the lower head fills with blood, the head on top of the shoulders loses its ability to think with the same rational clarity as before. Perhaps it's one reason that there's a preponderance of geriatric men on committees and in government. Younger men can't keep their minds focused on the mundane for long enough.

Then there's sexual desire or sex drive. The motivating force behind copulation. It certainly makes life interesting, although it's easy to argue that the desire factor is not only turned up way too high to merely guarantee the continuation of the species, but it goes on for way too long. People remain randy well beyond the age at which they can easily find attractive partners to hook up with. Partners whom they may have found extremely attractive some decades earlier. If the sexual attraction module was perfectly tuned we would all be attracted to partners of our own age. This would make everybody happier and would spare us from the scourge of pedophilia as well as the nauseating sight of wrinkly old billionaires with hot young trophies on their arms.

Drugs

There are a number of ways you can pimp your ride. You can add scoops and wings, big loud exhaust pipes, all manner of party lights, big wheels, small wheels, wide wheels, skinny wheels, racing stripes and full body wraps that change colour as the car moves.

Likewise, there are a number of ways to pimp your brain. Meaning drugs. Of the brain-altering variety. Aka recreational drugs. Drugs used for recreation as in relaxation and recreation, as in recreating the way your brain works and how the universe appears to be.

Recreational drugs include alcohol. It was a brilliant piece of marketing strategy to do whatever it took to normalise the phrase "drugs and alcohol", thus putting in the minds of the general public that whiskey is in the benign, legal, respectable category while marijuana, an infinitely less harmful drug, is in the dangerous, illegal, anti-social category. The bad guys (the booze, tobacco and guns complex) have always had the best spin doctors and lawyers.

Drugs are in the Good section because they can be fun. They also appear in the Bad section, because when they're bad, they're very, very bad.

Alcohol can be fun but it affects different brains in different

NOT VERY INTELLIGENT DESIGN THREE

ways. Some people become more entertaining while others are transformed into irrational punching machines after four pints of ale.

Psychedelics can be fun and can lead to a belief that you have seen God. You can experience being at one with nature and all things in the universe. Even though LSD is not addictive, non-lethal and harmless to those who don't have a pre-existing mental condition, those who have never experienced it are terrified of it and have made sure that it remains illegal for everybody else.

Drugs can also be the opposite of fun. The easiest way to learn about that is to ingest too much of any of them.

If you have too much marijuana, it can be extremely unpleasant, but you'll be feeling fine again as soon as the effects wear off, which doesn't take very long. A couple of hours at most.

If you have too much LSD you could experience almost anything good or bad that you could possibly imagine. No that's not right. You will experience all sorts of mad shit that you could never in a million years have imagined. Except maybe in dreams. But at least it won't kill you. And so long as your brain has no pre-existing tendency towards insanity, you'll be fine. All those stories about people jumping off buildings because they believe they can fly are much like the movie Reefer Madness. Bullshit and propaganda. Religious believers have always viewed psychedelics as a threat. Perhaps they worry that if people can experience God for themselves they'll have no appetite for a tithe-collecting mafia. The Spanish brutally suppressed the so-called mushroom cults in South America as they were a threat to the power of the Christian conquistadors. And for the gold.

If you have too much booze it's really, really unpleasant and it may take a few days for you to feel good again. Provided you haven't had enough to kill you. Isn't it amazing that a bottle of legal, respectable whiskey, if guzzled straight down, may quite possibly kill someone, yet there is no such thing as a lethal dose of marijuana. Alcohol is extremely addictive and has destroyed millions of lives.

If you have too much Oxycontin you may never be healthy again, and you are likely to vomit every time you see a picture of Richard Sackler or hear the Sackler name. In fact, Sackler-induced nausea can be experienced even by those who have never taken Oxycontin. A knowledge of what they did is enough to bring it on.

The topic of recreational drugs is way too big to try to deal with in this book so that wee tip o' the hat will have to do.

Rock 'n' Roll

Rock 'n' Roll is the heading because it naturally comes after sex and drugs, and completes the triple act of the most fun things healthy young adults can indulge in, although this bit also includes music of all types, as well as art in general.

Like sex and drugs, music is best when enjoyed with other people rather than alone. For most people this means live music events where the energy of the audience elevates the whole experience, including for the performers. For those lucky enough to have got together with friends in a band, the sensation of creating a new song, or playing something where everybody really fires together is akin to a simultaneous mental orgasm.

Art is its own reward, both for the creator and the audience. Even visual art can induce really powerful reactions. I didn't fully understand the expression "takes your breath away" until it happened to me. I had been enjoying the first few galleries in a Gerhard Richter exhibition at the Gallery of Modern Art in Brisbane, Australia, a few years ago, but was unprepared for the effect of three massive works on one wall in the next gallery. I stopped breathing. I thought I might be having a heart attack. Fortunately, there was a bench in the middle of the room. I sat down and gathered myself. I found it hard to believe that paintings could be so powerful.

The great thing about art, as opposed to sex and drugs, is

that there are very few harmful side effects. It's not unusual for great artists to succumb to booze or drugs or general madness, but it would be a bit of a stretch to blame that on the art, regardless of what a record sounds like when played backwards.

Love

Love is a wonderful thing. Whatever else makes you happy in life, you'll be even happier if you're also in love. In love with someone who's simultaneously in love with you, that is. Without the reciprocal bit it can be painful.

Love can also spark the worst in human behaviour. Jealousy and infidelity have triggered many a murder, quite a few wars and millions of bar fights.

But love isn't exclusive to the human animal. Look at the love dogs can have for humans. And vice versa. The internet is full of videos of inseparable animal couples, the pig and the miniature horse, the goose and the llama, the partridge and the pear tree. Such examples are arguably a purer form of love because there's no sexual element to it. At least we hope not. Although I'm guessing there are videos on the internet that would prove me wrong on that.

If it were an exclusively human thing, love would get a bigger mention here, but it's not, so we're moving on.

Dreams

Dreams can be brilliant or really annoying. Sometimes they go into a repetitive cycle, the same thing over and over, like you're trying to watch a game but you keep getting interrupted by the same commercial over and over again and the commercial is for the exact thing that you are at that moment trying to watch. Oh wait, that's not a bad dream, that's ESPN. I'm already watching the game you're advertising for fuck's sake! Why the fuck do you do that? What's the point of interrupting the game I'm watching to show me a promo for the exact fucking game I'm already fucking watching? Fuck off! Fuck all the way off! And keep fucking off. And when you get there, fuck off again.

The fact that people have become so dulled to the ever-present annoyance of TV ads says something about the faulty design of the human brain. But that has little to do with dreams so this isn't the place for that. An argument could also be made that it's a positive feature to be able to automatically tune out annoyances, so moving on.

Some dreams can be as wonderful as the greatest fantasy movie you've ever seen. Occasionally I've been lucky enough to have dreams that were in some ways visually similar to the movie What Dreams May Come, which was spectacular, but made less sense than most dreams. Though I saw it a long time ago so that could be wrong. Dreams don't really have full stories, they're like ads or trailers for something. Which may be why people try to find meaning in them. But seriously, trying to analyse things that are as chaotic and random as watching a video of a downhill cheese rolling race where someone keeps hitting the rewind button and then the forward button but the video is never quite the same as it was last time in either direction, seems like an exercise in futility.

The bad news is that you can only remember fleeting glimpses of them.

How the brain gets any rest when it spends most of the night in a four-dimensional theme park on acid is a mystery. This was almost in the section dealing with bad stuff because some people complain about nightmares, but I think the good dreams outnumber the bad ones. For me anyway. I enjoy most of my dreams. Except for when I dream I'm watching ESPN.

THE BAD

The Not Very Intelligent Bits

In contemplating the various attributes of the human brain and how they may be categorised, it was disappointing to discover that the category entitled The Good, aka The Intelligent Bits, was very much shorter than, The Bad, aka The Not Very Intelligent Bits.

The Bad, aka The Not Very Intelligent Bits is a massive list. It can be made a tad more wieldy by dividing it into The Bad, meaning merely not good, and The Ugly, meaning evil.

Actually it needs a further sub-division before we get that far. There are things that are bad about the human brain when it functions "normally" and things that are bad about the human brain when it has obvious defects. The sort of defect that were it to occur in an appliance, you'd know that you needed to call the repairman. Although these days you're more likely to just get a new appliance. Sadly that option is not yet available when it comes to human brains.

The segment about mental disorders will be brief on account of the fact that there's nothing humorous about mental disorders. At least not for decent, empathetic human beings and especially not for those who have to live with mental disorders, either in the same house, the same family or the same cranium. It also has to be brief because the tone of this book is essentially frivolous, which is inappropriate for serious subject matter. Tourettes. Shit. Fuck. Cock. Sorry.

Although this is an attempt to look at various aspects of the shortcomings of the human brain as separate things, it should always be remembered that whatever the particular disorder, it will rarely exist in isolation. There are lots of overlaps and lots of grey areas.

Mental Disorders

More than 12 percent of humans are born with some form of mental disorder. More than 25 percent of us will suffer from some form of mental problem at some time during our lives. If we are the perfect creations of God, made in his own image, does that mean that God has a few mental issues of his own? Given the often capricious and brutal treatment of his beloved flock as reported in the Old Testament, the answer is hell yes. His genocidal tendencies are a lot more than tendencies. He delights in a good massacre. So much so that he creates malignant narcissistic excuses for them. Bad humans made him do it. It was our fault. No surprises there.

Mental disorders, even at the mild end of the spectrum, make life extremely unpleasant for the afflicted. Life in this instance often means an entire life. From birth to death. Without respite. It can also mean the lives of family and friends.

Some mental disorders are the result of physical brain damage. People can be born with brain damage, it can be the result of an accident or the result of repeated concussion events. Other mental disorders can be caused by a chemical imbalance, or exposure to horrific events such as being raped, or witnessing the killing of every first born baby in a whole town. Or the My Lai massacre. Or being abused as a chid.

Even though "normal" is a state whose boundaries are not

universally agreed upon, those of us who fall into the "normal" category are lucky. I don't think it's too flippant to observe that we're all crazy, though some of us are less crazy than others. A similar thing applies to stupid, although where you draw that line is also subject to debate.

In 2020 the COVID-19 pandemic caused the number of people affected by anxiety and depressive disorders to spike by almost thirty percent. The sort of depression brought on by real world problems is not a kind of crazy, but is nevertheless a real mental disorder. We're all potentially just one random unfortunate event away from a mental meltdown.

This particular epoch has also raised the possibility that just as the communal intelligence of humanity grows, it may be possible that the planet could have a communal mental breakdown. The last few years have felt a lot like that.

The good news is that the medical profession is getting better at understanding and treating mental disorders. The bad news is that many disorders have the characteristic that the sufferer does not believe they have a problem which of course makes treatment impossible. The other thing that makes treatment impossible for many is a lack of money. Which can also be a contributing factor to depression.

I struggled with how to approach this section for so long that it was starting to have an effect on my mental health. So I decided not to write it at all. Writing about depression means thinking about depression which induces feelings of depression. Fuck that. So here's an incomplete list of things that qualify as mental disorders. They're all bad. Some are more than bad. Some are unspeakably horrible.

Bipolar disorder, depression, anxiety, anorexia, bulemia, obsessive compulsive disorder, schizophrenia, PTSD, ADHD, ASD, dissociative disorders, substance abuse, tourettes, dementia.

Information on these topics, and many more, is easily found on the internet. All that really needs saying is that if a creator deliberately designed all these things there is something extremely vile about that creator. Would a sane God design such things? Would a benevolent God design such things?

Personality Disorders

Although there's no clear line between Mental Disorders and Personality Disorders, mental disorders seem to be at the more serious end of the spectrum while some people can live their whole lives with a mild personality disorder without ever coming to the attention of a mental health professional. In fact they can live their lives without ever realising that they have a personality disorder. Just as someone who has been born into an isolated religious community thinks their situation as normal, someone with a rigid or unhealthy pattern of thinking sees their worldview as normal. It's all they've ever known.

That's not to say that personality disorders aren't serious. They really are. They can often be the difference between a life worth living and hell on earth.

If God created the human brain in his own image, then it stands to reason that there may be evidence in the bible that God is similarly afflicted by the disorders that afflict humans. Unfortunately, the Bible is far too boring to wade through to find examples of each and every one, but should they come to mind they'll be mentioned. The extreme narcissism of the first four commandments for example.

It's not surprising that the men who invented the character of the supreme ruler who made man "in his own image", wrote him as he appears in the old testament because that's what rulers who had absolute power over their subjects generally behaved like back then. And not only back then. All who attain absolute power tend to act like the megalomaniac in the Bible if they think they can get away with it. We haven't evolved much, certainly not noticeably, in the last three thousand years, and that unfortunately applies to our brains just as much as our bodies. Sure we've dramatically increased our total communal knowledge, but human evolution, whilst inexorable, is very, very slow. So our brains, with very few exceptions, still run HBOS (Human Brain Operating System) 1.01.

It would be impossible to be a despot without having **Narcissist Personality Disorder**. It's probably also impossible to rise to the top of anything that involves some sort of power over thousands of people without being a narcissist. Narcissism unsurprisingly comes in varying strengths with the worst of all being in combination with other traits known as the Dark Tetrad, as previously discussed.

ADD means Attention Deficit Disorder while **ADHD** means Attention Deficit Hyperactivity Disorder. They used to be used almost interchangeably. I have an attention deficit issue that involves nodding off to sleep whilst trying to do stuff on the computer after lunch, including trying to write things like this. There's no hyperactivity involved. Quite the opposite. Sometimes a nap is required. Sometimes the nap helps. Sometimes it doesn't. When children are diagnosed with ADHD they are often prescribed things like Ritalin which calms them down. Ritalin has the opposite effect on me, as it does for most adults. I took it once just for fun a few years ago and stayed up all night chatting to others in the same condition. It was pretty much indistinguishable from the powder we used to snort in order to drive trucks from London to Edinburgh and back again without sleeping, something that's no longer possible since technology killed the dual logbook method of long-distance lorry driving.

OCD is something I'm also slightly familiar with. When walking home from school I'd sometimes try to make sure that I stepped on an equal number of cracks with each foot. This would only occur if I was walking alone. Mostly I'd walk home with the other kids who lived nearby, in which case it wasn't even a thing. Thankfully. Some people can't leave home without going back to check that burners aren't left on or doors are locked. Pro tip. If you tap the lock three times it helps you remember whether you locked it or not. It's surprising that more old people aren't diagnosed with OCD because remembering stuff like that gets progressively more difficult as one ages. I suppose it requires an easy-going attitude that says, "Aah fuck it. If it burns down at least it's insured. Shit! Did I pay the insurance?"

Personality disorders are often grouped into clusters. They are called Cluster A, Cluster B and Cluster C. This is where the term clusterfuck originated. It really doesn't matter which or how many of these disorders you have, your life will be a clusterfuck. Then again it has a good chance of being a clusterfuck even if you don't have any of them. It depends on your location, family, workmates and friends. If they're all lunatics you have no chance. Run away.

The only redeeming feature of these personality disorders is the entertainment provided by watching experts trying to separate and classify each component of a sherry-filled trifle desert when they've have all helped themselves to a big serving of the trifle and had a few shots of sherry to wash it down. It's chaos. Just as you'd expect a big heaving jellybrain bobbing about in a cranium would be.

Clusterfuck A, according to the experts, are odd or eccentric ways of thinking or behaving. They include **paranoid personality disorder**, **schizoid personality disorder** and **schizotypal personality disorder**. Odd or eccentric? Jesus wept. If you've ever seen anybody in the midst of a paranoid or schizoid episode it's not odd or eccentric. It's fucking terrifying. Not from a concern about your own personal safety but from imagining the horror of what they appear to be going through. A living nightmare doesn't do it justice. Unless the nightmare is one hundred percent real, with one hundred percent real consequences. It's like they're in a trench watching their friends getting blown to pieces knowing that they'll be next.

Clusterfuck B includes dramatic, overly emotional or unpredictable thinking or behaviour. To be more clinical Clusterfuck B includes **antisocial personality disorder, borderline personality disorder, histrionic personality**

disorder and **narcissistic personality disorder**.

Antisocial Personality Disorder is exactly what it sounds like. Being a complete dickhead at all times, up to and beyond the level of criminality. Theft, violence, lack of remorse and total untrustworthiness, even to friends and family, are common features.

Borderline Personality Disorder includes the tendency to see everything as black and white. No grey areas. When somebody does something you don't like, that puts them on the bad side of the ledger and once someone is on the bad side, that's where they remain, never to be forgiven nor trusted again. This is hugely damaging to every type of relationship, especially families. It also involves impulsive and risky behaviour, such as having unsafe sex, gambling or binge eating, fragile self-esteem, unstable relationships, mood swings, and generally having a shitty, unhappy life.

Histrionic Personality Disorder involves making an absolute dick of yourself whenever you go out. Experts will never define it more accurately than the term Drama Queen, which applies equally to all genders, when applicable. Drama Queen has recently been replaced by the term "Karen" although Karens usually exhibit a fair dollop of racism to go with the rest of their unpleasant personality traits.

Narcissistic Personality Disorder is also part of Clusterfuck B. There are lots of ways to describe narcissists but generally speaking they're often not much fun to be around, and they naturally cluster with sycophants and other bottom munchers. A narcissist may refuse to speak to neighbours, friends or family members for days or weeks because of some perceived slight.

Clusterfuck C includes the anxious and fearful disorders. They're called **Avoidant Personality Disorder, Dependent Personality Disorder** and **Obsessive-compulsive Personality Disorder** which is apparently not the same as obsessive-compulsive disorder, which is a type of anxiety disorder.

All of which is bringing on a case of ADD in my brain (aka getting a bit bored), hence the abbreviated ending to this bit.

Inflexible Thinking is not generally referred to as a personality disorder, but it's very much like one. Unsurprisingly it's a condition characterised by an unwillingness to change one's mind. Those who suffer from rock brain (which is the literal translation for the German term for the condition) see it as a strength of character that they can stick to their guns, though people who have to live with, or work with them, see it as a pain in the ass. Even with the arrival of new information which clearly indicates the benefits of a change of approach, inflexible thinkers will stick to their original decision.

Inflexible thinking may be a symptom of one or more mental health conditions, such as obsessive-compulsive disorder, autism spectrum disorder, and some personality disorders. It may also be a result of learned behaviour, such as rigid parenting styles or exposure to cultural or societal norms that emphasise conformity.

If the human brain was programmed by God, why did he think it was a good idea to create so many absolutely horrible brain distortion apps?

Memory

If you had to pick the single most important function of the human brain it would be hard to go past memory. Or maybe...aaah, what was that other thing?... nah, memory. Definitely memory.

Anyone who has some experience with an Alzheimers sufferer knows that human beings cease to function without memory. If you can't remember where home is, you'll never find your way back there and even if you do, you'll always be alone, because you don't know anybody any more. If you can't remember how to feed yourself, you will die. Unless there's someone there to feed you.

So a memory that fails is the worst thing that can happen to somebody. Fortunately, unlike eyes that fail in almost everybody, severe memory failure or dementia afflicts a minority and usually only occurs very late in life. From the age of about 70, your chances of losing your marbles increases steadily. If you make it to 90, you have about a one in five chance of forgetting who you are.

You won't be able to leave your house because if you do you'll be the dude that doesn't know where his car is parked. But that happens about the same time that you can't remember how to drive it, so there's that. And a self driving Tesla won't help much. Your phone will know where the car is, and the car will know where home is, but even if you haven't lost your phone, will you remember where the app is? Or what an app is? The sad part of this situation is that when the memory goes, so does all meaning in life.

As an aside, we should recognise the need to end the suffering of those so afflicted. Having seen the painful, bewildered suffering of my mother for the last five years of her life, there should have been an act of mercy available for her and for all those who suffer as she did. One day we'll look back and realise that we were in the habit of giving mercy to our beloved pets many decades before allowing the same relief to our beloved elders. It's okay to be humane to your animals but it's illegal to be humane to your humans.

Even in healthy brains with fully functioning memories, it turns out that the human memory is a very buggy piece of storage equipment. It's about as reliable as an old Fiat. We often think we have a reasonable memory, but evidence can turn up that makes you question that. Such as a photograph of you with a good friend in a far away place but you can't remember having been there, or at least not with them. When you talk with friends or family about an event that happened a few years previously it's not unusual to discover that everyone recalls it slightly, or even very, differently.

The hippocampus is not a place of higher learning for Pablo Escobar's abandoned pets, it's the place in the brain where the hard drive is. Where the new memories get stored. Just why it was named after hippos rather than elephants, when elephants are well known to be the kings of memory, is a morsel of knowledge that seems to have been forgotten.

Memories can not only be erased, they can be implanted. Researchers have been able to convince people that they remember being involved in crimes many years earlier. Other experts have managed to convince hundreds or thousands of children that they have been the victims of satanic ritual abuse in child care centres. After the incarceration of a number of the alleged perpetrators, it took years for the truth to emerge. The truth being that these events, never took place, except for in the imaginations of the experts, and then the children who they were supposedly helping.

We are learning to rely less on eye-witness testimony as it becomes clear that the hippocampi of the witnesses are recording things to memory that might be imagined or partially imagined and things that are vague, and therefore susceptible to change by suggestive reinforcement of false recall. Hundreds of convicted criminals have been exonerated and set free by DNA evidence. In 70 percent of those cases, they were convicted partially or wholly on the basis of eye-witness evidence. The witnesses weren't lying. In most cases, that is. They thought they were recalling things accurately, but they were wrong.

In one case an expert witness convinced a judge and jury to visit the scene of a drive-by shooting at a time when ambient light conditions were the same as at the time of the crime. Although the witnesses positively identified the alleged shooter, a recreation of the drive-by demonstrated that it was impossible to identify anybody in the car. Were the witnesses lying? Doubtful. They had no reason to lie. Were they mistaken? Yes. After they found out who the suspects were, mug shots filled in the blanks where their memories weren't. Had the judge refused to make that journey to the scene it's fairly certain that an innocent man (he had an alibi) would have spent the rest of his life in prison.

Memory is also essential in order to plan the future. If you have no idea about what's happened before, you have nothing on which to base future plans. No way of improving on previous outcomes or the design of things.

It's lucky we figured out how to write things down, because that's how we developed a communal memory, and only with a comprehensive communal memory can we make progress. Imagine trying to design a passenger jet using only the knowledge in your brain if that knowledge consisted only of information that had been passed on verbally. It would be a task beyond the capability of the world's greatest engineer with the world's best memory. In fact there would be no substantial buildings, no power grid, no running water, no roads, no cars, nothing of any substance would be possible, without a written record of our communal memory.

If you have no idea about what's happened before, you not only have nothing on which to base future plans, you have no way of avoiding previous mistakes. Those who are ignorant of history are doomed to repeat it, as the saying goes. It's important for the future of humanity to have an accurate record of our history. The most evil despots always try to rewrite history for their own benefit. It's the equivalent of brainwashing everybody simultaneously, or bashing everyone's brains in with a baseball bat.

An accurate, truthful record of history, unable to be altered over time, is arguably the most important thing humanity could possess. Some form of properly authenticated historical Wikipedia on a blockchain would be far more valuable than a digital baseball card NFT. Perhaps a communal memory-themed ICO could be floated.

Memory can occasionally be superhuman. Like that guy who can take a helicopter ride around Manhattan then sit down and draw the whole thing. Perfectly. Every building where it should be. Normal brains can't imagine how that could be possible. We wouldn't even be aware of seeing every building let alone remember them. Or those musical savants who can hear a complex piece of music just once, then perform it perfectly. Sadly such spectacular brain function is many orders of magnitude rarer than stupid brains. Which are damn near everywhere.

If the brain of man was a creation of God, then he did very a poor job of ensuring the integrity of its most important function. We all live our lives with a lot less than total recall. "If I'm not me then who the hell am I?"

Stupidity

The human brain is the command and control centre of the human animal. Its primary function is to keep itself, along with the rest of the body, operational, healthy and safe. When the brain fails to function perfectly the results can vary from a twitch to a stutter to a heart attack to a car crash to an alcohol overdose to suicide.

Although other parts of the human anatomy, such as the immune system, play big parts in the survival game, brain health also affects subconscious and unconscious functions. As evidenced by psychosomatic illness and the placebo effect on what should be a purely physical situations.

Also when the brain dies, every other part of the body shuts down.

If death is at one end of a spectrum and intelligence at the other, then stupidity falls somewhere in between.

As well as keeping the body functioning by operating the organs on autopilot, an intelligent brain is required to make conscious decisions to keep the body alive by doing such things as avoiding bears, not stepping off tall buildings, not playing in traffic and not eating poop.

Humans are very slow learners when compared to other animals who can walk within moments of their birth. Not only are we slow to learn, human babies are so likely to accidentally harm themselves that their parents are effectively on 24/7 suicide watch for the first few years of a baby's life. Toddlers will discover ways to electrocute themselves, throw themselves out of windows, drown themselves and cover themselves with boiling water unless someone is there to stop them. Should an infant brain manage to survive for a few years, that brain can at last turn itself to more complicated tasks than trying to shove every small thing within reach into its mouth. The habit of trying to prevent self-harm has to be learned. That it's not more instinctive for young humans is not intelligent design.

Provided the brain functions normally for all automatic organic functions and not cause things like never ending hiccups, impromptu swearing, clumsiness or an inability to turn left, that leaves what we mostly think of as the brain's real job. Making intelligent decisions. Intelligent decisions are not a great challenge for an intelligent brain.

Intelligence is distributed like so many other things along a spectrum. Just like attractiveness and ugliness, there are a small number of people who are almost unbelievably intelligent, and some who are unbelievably thick. The main problem from the point of view of the brain being designed by a creator is that the creator put the peak of the bell curve towards the stupid end of the spectrum. If you meet someone who has been described in advance as being of average intelligence you will understand this easily. If you can't identify the stupidest person in the conversation, it could well be you.

This hadn't been much of a problem in years gone by as stupid people didn't have a voice and were often resigned to the idea that it was their lot to go uncomplainingly down the mine every day. But then came the internet. And social media. And with it the amplification of stupidity.

Previously there were gatekeepers to regulate outbursts of amplified public stupidity. For example the people who read the letters to the editor and decided which ones were worthy of being published. Which voices were not too absurd to be heard. Speakers Corner in London was the place for unfettered free speech. Anyone could get on a soap box and say anything they wanted to. It became well known as a place to go and have a laugh at the expense of the crazy and stupid. Alex Jones and Piers Morgan would have been regulars had they been born a generation or two earlier.

As the voices of the stupid became more prevalent, more stupid people became aware of them and found, unsurprisingly, that they agreed with them. Malign influences such as Talkcrap Radio and Faux News recognised the value, meaning the financial value, of broadcasting far-fetched conspiracy theories and narrow minded bigotry, and the stupid came to believe that their views were just as valuable as the views of intelligent people. After all it was what people were saying on the radio and on TV. And the internet.

And so came the rise of alternate facts, and the idea that both sides of an argument have equal value. Which is of course dangerous nonsense. If one side is the truth and the other side is a lie, why should they be given equal air time? Should a debate on whether the earth is flat or spherical or some other shape or form, be on prime time with a panel of four "experts" on each side? No. It shouldn't be on the air at all, because it's just a stupid waste of time that encourages idiots to believe nonsense. And become more likely to believe further nonsense. Should an obvious lie be given equal air time to a verifiable fact?

The "both sides" thing is a deliberate propaganda tool designed to foment disruption and dissent. Ten stupid people are not smarter than one smart person. They are ten times as stupid, on account of their reinforced and amplified belief in stupid ideas, as well as their willingness to enforce their stupidity on others by means of violence.

All of which is not meant to imply that the world was a wonderful, better or even good place before the rise of the morons. Not at all. The world was a terrible place, because smart or privileged people with power and limited empathy or malign intent can do a hell of lot more damage and inflict a whole lot more misery on people, than a horde of intellectually challenged proles.

The Dunning-Kruger effect

Put simply, the Dunning Kruger Effect is the observation that an intelligent, educated individual has a fairly good idea about the size and scope of a subject and therefore has a pretty good idea of how much they know about. Which means they also understand how much they don't know about it. Stupid people on the other hand have no idea at all about how much they don't know, and are therefore likely to assume that what they do know is a reasonable chunk of what there is to know.

People who score 90% or more in exams often estimate their results within two or three points of their actual score, mostly erring on the low side. This is because they know what they got right and don't add anything for correct guesses. People who score 70 - 80% will usually be fairly close to their estimate (but not as close), whereas many of those who predict they will score 50 or 60%, in fact get 30 - 40%. They have little idea how much they don't know or understand about the subject.

This should not be misunderstood as mere ignorance of a topic rather than stupidity, because an intelligent person is usually aware that there may be a great deal more to a given topic whereas a stupid person is unlikely to even consider such a concept. When a stupid person hears a group of stupid people expressing stupid opinions that they happen to agree with, it reinforces their belief that they know enough about the subject to have a solid and correct opinion about it.

Although lack of intelligence is one of the major handbrakes on the path to a better world, not all misguided thinking can be attributed to lack of intelligence. In some cases, otherwise intelligent people can be totally convinced of the veracity of something as ludicrous as Scientology for example. Or Mormonism. Or conspiracy theories.

Unfortunately not all conspiracy theories are completely crazy, or even wrong, which just complicates things. Although a blanket distrust of vaccines requires some combination of stupidity, ignorance and crazy, given that vaccines have largely eradicated such terrible diseases as Smallpox, Polio, Tetanus, Hepatitis, Rubella, Measles and Whooping Cough. The worst part of that particular crazy is that measles and whooping cough are staging a resurgence in some parts of the world thanks to the crystal gazing, homeopathic, natural immunity experts on social media and the idiots who believe them. Correction. The worst part is that the actions of the dangerously stupid also puts the lives of others in jeopardy.

Stupid people can take the credit for many thousands of deaths due to thinking that someone on Facebook knows more about vaccines than the scientists who create them.

As George Carlin said there's stupid, full of shit and fuckin' nuts. He also said there are a huge number of stupid people out there. He estimated he met thirty or forty really stupid people every day. He said, "Think of how stupid the average person is, and half the people are stupider than that."

Many people have problems such as dyslexia that make it hugely difficult for them to learn to read. Others just never manage to learn, perhaps because of their social circumstances, perhaps they're just slow learners, but whatever it is the statistics are scary. 21% of adults in the USA are functionally illiterate. That means unable to write a shopping list or read street signs. One in five. Twenty or thirty in every movie theatre. No wonder subtitled movies aren't very popular.

When you consider that the single thing that separates humanity from all other animals is our ability to communicate, it follows that there is nothing more important for a human to learn than the language (whichever language applies to your region) that we use to communicate.

54% of adults in the United States read at level of sixth grade or below. Sure, that's enough to be a fully functional member of society, but it's not something to be proud of. It also corresponds with George Carlin's observation.

Not long after a drunk doctor in Texas showed his friend that his Tesla could go from zero, to holy shit, to tree, to fireball in three point two seconds, a few mask-free anti-vaxxers, in an attempted hold my beer moment, were seen on social media preparing for an imminent gasoline price hike by pumping the lethal liquid into large plastic bags in the trunks of their cars.

Consumer Reports got into the game of telling Tesla horror stories by tricking a Tesla into driving itself along the road by means of a weight on a chain hanging from the steering wheel. Had it escaped their notice that you can trick any modern car into moving forward at a life threatening speed by engaging cruise control then climbing into the passenger seat? Or even any older car by using a stick or brick to depress the accelerator pedal? Did they at no point ask, what exactly are we trying to prove here? That it's possible to do really stupid things that are suicidally dangerous?

Consumer Reports however were rewarded for their efforts with a massive increase in website clicks, and so were emboldened to try harder. News of four fatalities attributed to morons trying to emulate their driverless car video prompted a board meeting. Board member Madeleine Notbryte was reported in the minutes as saying, "Four deaths for two hundred thousand clicks. That's a price we think is worth paying. Besides, it's not as if we knew any of them." Although Consumer Reports had not in fact paid any of the idiots who killed themselves in the quest for their own social media clicks, they did come up with a plan to pay the poor and desperate for performing stupidly dangerous acts using the justification that it was no different from drug companies who paid the poor and desperate for ingesting drugs with potentially dangerous side effects.

Consumer Reports initiated a project codenamed "All Hands on Deck", whose aim was to scare the bejeebus out of everyday consumers by demonstrating that normal household appliances could be ridiculously dangerous if used in ridiculously dangerous ways. First they tricked a kitchen blender into making a Bloody Mary out of a volunteer's left hand. The Consumer Reports staff reported that the human guinea pig did not appear to show any pain. They admitted later that they had not drug tested the volunteers as they suspected that none of them would pass any sort of sobriety test and they had click targets to pursue. For the same video another volunteer sacrificed a hand to the Insinkerator in the staff kitchen. For this trick they tossed a dime bag into the device which was already spinning at top speed. The volunteer was wearing a pair of Beats headphones turned up to eleven, which may have been a contributing factor. Only after Madeleine and the rest of the board were shown the disgusting video of a volunteer's hand cooked medium rare in a George Foreman grill, did Consumer Reports pull the plug on the project.

It's not always so easy to tell what's real and what's a ridiculous exaggeration when it comes to stupid things that stupid people do. "Internet challenges" often involve people doing stupid and dangerous things (such as swallowing household poisons and setting themselves on fire) for 15 seconds of fame if they're lucky, and/or permanent disability or sometimes even death, if they're not.

The worst part about stupid is that it can't be fixed. This is so widely accepted that there has never been any scientific effort made to even attempt to fix stupid. Sadistic school teachers used to try to beat the stupid out of children, which only resulted in fertilising any violent tendencies already present in the stupid ones.

Delusion and Gullibility

Movies often come with an on-screen disclaimer declaring them to be fiction and that any resemblance to actual persons living or dead is entirely coincidental. This is mostly an attempt to avoid lawsuits of the defamation type whether legitimate or imagined but is also evidence of the tendency for people to believe that what they're being told is true, even in a place where works of fiction are the norm.

It's one small piece of a mountain of evidence that we are gullible by nature. We're generally happy to simply believe what we're told. Had our brains been set to a position closer to the sceptical end of the dial we'd arguably be a lot better off. We wouldn't be hamstrung by a refusal to believe anything, but we would be free of the handbrake of organised religion and free from the poison of snake oil which charlatans are always happy to sell us.

Another piece of evidence is the flood of emails that are sent everyday to encourage people to claim easy millions that have been held up at airports or some other part of the delivery system. Not all of these originate from Nigeria. Many of them come from the CIA, the FBI, the Royal Banking Lottery Commission of Amsterdam, the Elon Musk Lucky Millionaire prize draw fund, etcetera. Many of them are from people who have millions of dollars, but an unfortunate inability to transfer those millions anywhere without access to your account details. They are obviously scams, not only for the risible B-movie plot lines, but also for the lack of attention to detail regarding spelling and grammar, address details and the like. Who could possibly fall for them? Quite a lot of people apparently.

The most alarming thing to learn about this type of phishing is that the obviousness of their scammy nature is deliberate. They're not looking for people of even average intelligence. Intelligent people would waste their time, perhaps going along with the scam for a few days or weeks and then getting cold feet and never actually parting with any money. No, the phishermen are after the truly gullible, those at the more stupid end of the spectrum. The apparent stupidity of the phishing letter is in fact a filter. Smart people need not apply.

How gullible are we naturally? Is gullibility learned?

It's often said that we'd be better served if there was more emphasis placed on critical thinking skills at all levels of education. We'd certainly be better at making decisions to avoid becoming victim to grifters. The problem is that critical thinking skills are anathema to persons and organisations who have an interest in controlling a compliant group of people. Persons such as those who run churches or other multi-level schemes that peddle different brands of essential snake oils.

If a person of average intelligence received a full education except for anything about gods and religion, what are the chances they would find any religion plausible when learning about it for the first time as an adult? Hard to say. It's true that some adults swap one religion for another, so anything's possible, but the numbers of the faithful would surely be greatly diminished.

Which is why churches love to run schools. They say it's important to teach children things such as morality and virtue and fear of God. The real reason churches run schools is because they know that if they brainwash the young into believing, there's a good chance that they'll continue to believe and give money to the church for the rest of their lives. (Another reason that churches run schools is that if your organisation contains a large number of pedophiles then what's better than schools? Boarding schools? Yes. Orphanages? Perfect. But that's a digression. We're talking about gullibility here, not the rampant pedophilia found in religious groups.) The last thing churches want are students with well developed critical thinking skills. This is why the extremely pious often resort to book burning and trying to close libraries.

Lots of young people lose their religion when they go to college. Not because they become corrupted by the devil weed, but because they spend a whole lot of time talking with open-minded intelligent peers. Any open-minded discussion of the Bible cannot help but reveal the absurdity therein.

Schools aren't the only places that can increase levels of

gullibility. Pharmacies (at least where I live in New Zealand) have whole sections dedicated to homeopathy. Aka pseudoscience. Pharmacists are scientists. At least they should be. They have to study a fair bit of science in order to become a pharmacist. Yet when it comes to selling wellbeing, they're happy to push snake oil to their gullible patrons. Most of them must know what they're doing. Sure, there'll be a few loonies amongst them, who'll believe that a single drop of alcohol in an ocean will be enough to inebriate a whole team of Navy Seals, but most of them are just happy to take the suckers' cash. Homeopathy has as much chance of curing disease as a piano with no keys, hammers or strings has of playing Bohemian Rhapsody.

Alternative medicine is a title that endows itself with an elevated sense of importance. It's not a valid alternative to conventional medicine, it's not a branch of scientific medicine, it's woo woo. It's nonsense that somebody just made up. Somebody with the ethical standards of a Nigerian phisherman.

Some ancient traditional medicines do actually work, although ascribing their efficacy to some mystical, spiritual forces of the elders is a mistake. The reason they work is that they've evolved over a long period of time using the scientific method known as trial and error. If you rub this plant on that infection it will help it to heal. Other plants have been tried and proven ineffective, harmful or deadly. We pass on this knowledge to our children. Our forefathers have known it since the beginning of time. Or for a few generations at least.

Anecdotal evidence is accepted to some degree by most people, even though we all (should) understand that a single event is of no value when compared to properly gathered statistical data involving thousands of events. My neighbour rubbed a ferret on her warts and it cured them. Wow, really? Where can I get a ferret? They sell them at the chemist shop between the homeopathic suppositories and the thigh magnets.

Flat earthers. Do any of them really believe the earth is flat? The observable physical evidence is so overwhelming that I suspect most of them are just having a laugh. Then again a similar argument applies to lots of stupid shit that people believe, so who knows?

Urban Legends

Just as we humans are prone to accept anecdotes of uncertain origin as evidence of things like dangerous vaccines, spontaneous combustion or medicinal miracles, we are also big fans of "urban legends", even when the story takes place nowhere near an urban area. Such as the aerial fire bombing plane that picked up a scuba diver and dropped him into the forest, where he was impaled atop a tall tree. Many scary beast stories are commonly retold featuring Bigfoot, the Loch Ness Monster, the Beast of Bodmin Moor, The Beast of Exmoor, the Hound of the Baskervilles, the Bunny Man, the Highgate Vampire, the Mad Gasser of Mattoon, the Burly Bald Bastard of Badcock, the Miserable old Milk Maid of Meenie Moor and many more.

There is no credible evidence that any of the above are true although some are less implausible than others.

The Curse of the Half Fly Fly Half. During a quarter final match in the 1932 World Cup of Rugby, one of the players jerked convulsively as he kicked the ball in an effort to initiate a dubious tactic known as the defensive box kick. The player, Farnie DeRieur of South Africa, hit the ground writhing and waving his arms as the game carried on without him, as is the norm in the sport of big manly men. When the opposition team finally scored, an almost inevitable result of the near vertical box kick, the players returned to the stricken player who was, by this time, dead. A post mortem revealed that he had choked to death on a fly, or more accurately half a fly, as evidenced by the other half of the fly lodged between his teeth and lower lip. It was deemed that the fly had entered his mouth at a crucial moment just as the player closed his mouth to kick the ball, then inhaled for the very last time immediately thereafter.

The incident would almost certainly have disappeared into the mists of time had the coroner not quipped that to die of half a fly was a hell of a way for a fly half to die. To this day it has been the custom at every World Cup of Rugby for the rest of the team, before each game, to say to the fly half (also known as the scrum half or half back), "Keep your mouth shut, mate!"

The Curse of the Half Fly Fly Half would arguably rank a lot higher on the table of infamous curses had Farnie DeRieur not been the only fly half, or in fact the only rugby player, make that the only anybody, to have ever died in this manner. The customary recitation of "Keep your mouth shut, mate", is not linked in any way to the theatrical tradition of saying "break a leg" instead of "good luck" before a performance. Contrary to popular belief, the phrase, "Hope you drown today, you bastard", is never used by yachtsmen either to their own crew, or to opposing crews, before any regatta, although many people have said that Dennis Connor has been known to mutter such things.

A rocket powered car with the rear end protruding from the side of a mountain has never been photographed just as a team of drunk men have never been caught on video successfully tipping a sleeping cow onto its side. This is probably due to the fact that cows prefer to sleep lying down.

Often introduced as a true story is the tale of a belligerent battleship that makes increasingly serious threats to another vessel to change course until the other vessel reveals that it is in fact a lighthouse. This urban legend/joke was recently updated by the Ukrainian military who responded to similar threats from a Russian warship with the evergreen classic, "Go fuck yourself."

Hitchhikers are the subject of many urban legends, often as victims, sometimes as perpetrators, and invariably as ghosts who prey on drivers and/or hitchhikers.

The Celebrity Cryogenic Centre in the desert of New Mexico houses cryostasis chambers that contain, among other things, the body of Walt Disney, the brain of JFK, the arms of Babe Ruth, the vocal cords of Dean Martin, and the genitalia of Hugh Hefner. A reservation has been placed for the butthole of (insert preferred punchline character here).

The Celebrity Death Rule of Threes is a superstition that movie stars, celebrities, and politicians die in groups of three. Tik Tok influencers and celebrity fans often search and scroll without pause for up to three days after two famous people die in quick succession, hoping to be first to post about the third death. If no further death occurs within three days they revert to scrolling aimlessly as usual and forget all about it.

The Boston Red Sox' failure to win The World Series for 86 years (1918 to 2004) was superstitiously attributed to The Curse of the Bambino. The Bambino was the nickname of Babe Ruth, who was sold to the New York Yankees in 1920, and whose arms lie in waiting for a new slugger in the Celebrity Cryogenic Centre.

Project MKUltra was the birth place of the urban legend that involved people ingesting LSD then jumping to their deaths because they believed they could fly. It is true that the CIA funded program that ran from the early 1950s to the early 1970s was responsible for many dangerous, irresponsible, and inhumane experiments on American citizens and in fact may have caused enough mental damage to some participants that the easiest way to shut them up was to throw them out of tall buildings, but as far as tripping hippies performing the death leap voluntarily, there is no plausible account.

El Trauco is a repulsive dwarf-like creature with hypnotic powers that is known to prey on and impregnate unmarried women in the woods of Chiloé Island in the south of Chile. Women are helpless to resist his magnetic allure and when encountering him will immediately begin to fornicate with him. Single, pregnant women are considered blameless because everyone knows the repulsive dwarf-like creature is irresistible. I'm not making this up. (Although someone else obviously did.) Perhaps because such pregnancies are relatively common, the babies are not considered to be the offspring of God and are therefore unlikely to be worshipped or crucified. The woman does of course require cleansing, and a marriage is believed to achieve that.

Shit vs Shinola

Whether it's an extended warranty, a multi-level marketing scheme that encourages you to buy a garage full of shit that you'll never be able to resell, a ponzi scheme disguised as a complex financial instrument, an alien abduction, a device to keep your brain safe from 5G radiation, or the nonsense that Deepak Chopra spews about the moon being an indefinable quantum soup that switches on and off at the speed of light, people have great difficulty distinguishing shit from Shinola.

Not all shit is easy to tell from Shinola. Newspaper reports about the state of the economy can vary from honest to outright lies, and yet still be hard to evaluate. If it mentions trickle down economics and tax cuts for the wealthy it's easy to call bullshit, but long term financial debt ceilings and a favourable free trade deal are anybody's guess.

Responsible democratic governments try to look after their citizens by means of consumer protection agencies, but where there's money, there'll always be conmen and charlatans.

(For non-Americans, the colloquial phrase, "You wouldn't know shit from Shinola," refers to a once famous brand of boot polish that died in 1960. Shit means the same thing in America as it does elsewhere, although "He's the shit," may mean "he's the best", whereas "he's shit" just means he's shit. I hope that clarifies things.)

Cults and shared delusions

What's the difference between a cult and a religion?

The number of adherents.

That sounds flippant, but is it untrue?

Their commonality includes a requirement to believe some totally implausible nonsense that someone made up, follow some silly rules that someone made up, and to give money, and sometimes all your earthly possessions, to someone who claims to represent some spiritual being or cause.

Possible differences may be that cults are smaller and newer and may still have the founder in place.

In either case the founder often has a rule, generally unwritten, that he is entitled, if not obliged, to have sex with every member of his flock that takes his fancy, whether or not they are already married, whether adult or child. In the case of the Bible, God asserted his right to impregnate a married virgin. A story that is obviously true because who else but God could have found a married virgin in Nazareth, or Jerusalem, or Bethlehem or wherever she was when the spirit moved inside her. Was Mary pregnant for nine months, or was it more miraculous than that? Was the baby, who was already God, able to walk, talk or do anything special in his first few months and years of life as a sort of human?

Apparently not. Why not?

Wouldn't it have been more impressive for God's son to have appeared as a fully-formed, bearded preacher-man in an explosive, meteoric arrival, robes blazing, booming like a Falcon 9 touching down on LZ-1 at Cape Canaveral? Marvel Comic characters can do it.

But God sent a baby. (It's probably not surprising that Jesus was unable to do anything superhuman for the early years of his life as that tracks with God's inability to do anything supernatural since the invention of the video camera.)

People join cults in the hope of finding unconditional love, a sense of community, of belonging, a family and for the really needy, a home, often provided by a communal settlement environment. As soon as you arrive in a cult compound the brainwashing begins. Although brainwashing is actually the opposite - it doesn't mean cleaning things out so much as filling the brain with fantastical stories and giving any existing sense of normality a sound beating which is reinforced with a physical regime that may include long work days and sleep deprivation.

Perhaps the reason that most small cults remain small is that many of their members were recruited and indoctrinated as adults rather than as children which is far more effective in establishing life-long faith. If a cult can hold onto its membership for two generations they may emerge from the cocoon and become a church, with a self-regenerating congregation.

To outsiders it's obvious that cult members are not in a normal, rational state of mind. They appear to be under a spell. Ex-cult members have described the feeling of being dragged into the vortex, of feeling the irresistible power of the draw of the cult, but having no idea of exactly how or why it happened to them.

In his book The Cult of Trump, Steven Hassan, a former Moonie, draws parallels between Trump and people like Jim Jones, David Koresh, Ron Hubbard, and Sun Myung Moon. Hassan describes the ways that people become loyal and obedient through techniques of social psychology.

Former Trump lawyer and bag man, Michael Cohen, described himself as a demented follower of Trump. He said he fell under a trance-like spell. "Around Trump I felt excited, alive, like he possessed the urgent and only truth, the chance for my salvation and success in life," Cohen wrote. "That is what it feels like to lose control of your mind - you actually give up your common sense, sense of decency, sensitivity, even your grip on reality. I was in a cult of personality. And I loved it."

Most people, at some time in their lives, consider the questions, "Why am I here?", "What's the purpose of life?", "What's the purpose of my life?", "There must be some meaning, there's gotta be a reason for it all, how did it begin?", "Why did it begin?", etcetera. The problem with such questions is that the only sensible answer is, "I don't know".

Not only is it the only sensible answer, it's the only truthful answer, as there's no way of knowing if there's even a possibility that a definitive answer will ever be discovered. That we arrived here as a result of cosmic coincidence and billions of years of evolution with no reason or purpose is, for most people, not as satisfying as a big dollop of woo woo infused bullshit. That's a shame but it seems to be how our not so intelligent brains are wired. All other answers are shit that people have simply made up. Out of whole cloth as the saying goes.

Some of the ridiculous ideas and fables that cults and religions are based on are more risible than others. Despite being large and powerful enough to be a religion, Scientology is still widely thought of as a cult. Except for the IRS who were cowed into granting tax-free church status to Scientology after a brilliant campaign of harassment by Scientologists who conspired to overwhelm the IRS with a tsunami of frivolous filings. Other nations have tax departments not so easily bullied.

L Ron Hubbard wrote the books on Scientology after honing his craft on pulp sci-fi novels. It is said that Hubbard once proclaimed, "If you want to make real money, start a religion." Whether he actually said that or not, there's a lot more truth in it than in any of the old bollocks that Scientologists are supposed to believe as part of their religion.

Elron wasn't the only one to see the value in the big lie. Joseph Goebbels was an expert propagandist and a big fan of the big lie. Although there doesn't seem to be proof that he actually said it, he's often credited with, "If you tell a lie big enough and keep repeating it often enough, people will eventually come to believe it."

And then you can get them to do anything. As Voltaire supposedly said or wrote (once again solid attribution is hazy), "Those who can make you believe absurdities can make you commit atrocities." History is jam-packed with examples of religiously inspired atrocities.

Churches are the richest organisations on earth. They have branches in every town in every country on earth, righteously and routinely bleeding the poor and offering nothing in return but lies and false hope. The human brain needs answers, and any answer, no matter how crazy, is apparently better than uncertainty, even when uncertainty is the only truthful answer.

We'd rather put our faith in a lie than have no faith at all. Some may argue that God programmed us to require faith, to require belief in God, but the programming is clearly faulty, because we do not gravitate to the one true God, rather we believe in all manner of false gods.

If God designed the human brain and then commanded us to worship him and no other, then clearly the human brain is a not very intelligently designed.

Prayer, Superstition and the Paranormal

Prayer is a bit like buying a lottery ticket in that it provides a sense of hope. The main difference is that you might win the lottery.

Some people devote a lot of time to prayer, despite it being the single least effective thing ever invented by humankind. If you think that's an unfair characterisation, let's calculate the number of prayers answered (definitely and unmistakably) divided by the number of prayers prayed. That would be zero, divided by billions, equals zero. Orders of magnitude of zeroness.

Professional athletes can often be seen making physical gestures to their god above after a victory or scoring a goal or whatever. If the final score is three two, then God gets five thank you prayers. Do they ever ask themselves in the locker room before kick off which side god will be on today? Doubtful. God is always on the side of anyone who scores and if one team loses, well that's just mysterious. There must be a reason, because God will always do what's best.

So what's the origin of prayer. Where did prayer come from? Prayer rhymes with fear. That's probably a coincidence, although there is a strong correlation between the two. People pray when they are scared. When a cyclone shakes the roof, people pray. When the boat they're on sails into big unruly swells, people pray. When clear air turbulence makes it feel like the wings might fall off, people pray. When it hasn't rained for a month and the crops begin to fail, people pray.

Thunder, lightning, earthquakes and volcanoes are all terrifying and all result in prayers to make them stop. Perhaps gods were invented out of post fear-prayer embarrassment. Who were you talking to? Yourself? Are you crazy? No, I was praying to the god who made the wind.

It's said by religious folk that there are no atheists in foxholes. Even if that were true, which is extremely doubtful, what's it supposed to show? That terrified people pray? We know that. Perhaps that's why God created terrorists? What it really illustrates is that many people of faith can't get to grips with the idea that it's possible to live a life free of the fear of God. Would a moment of intense fear cause a person to reassess their belief in Santa Claus?

Urging inanimate or unhearing objects to do something is a common human trait. Shouting at a computer to work properly or at a traffic jam to get out of the way for example.

Curlers do a lot of shouting, mostly at each other. They shout at each other to sweep, to sweep harder and to stop sweeping, which is often the loudest shouting of all. This is the reason the sport is popular among spectators. Especially the mixed doubles, where married couples compete at the highest level. Watching them shouting at each other before calmly debriefing after the curl is excellent entertainment.

And a good life lesson for all married couples. It's also entertaining when the tension reaches a level such that they won't look at each other after a good shouting.

Curlers also shout at the curling stones. Urging them to travel in a more favourable direction. This is akin to praying to thunder to stop, although in both cases if there is no invocation to a god, there is no conscious expectation that it will achieve anything. Curlers have sometimes been caught on a close-up camera shot finger praying. Finger prayer is when you cross fingers in the belief that it will bring the result you desire. Sounds a little wacky, but statistics show that it is just as effective as praying to any of the more established gods.

Unlike the shouting in curling, golf has been made a lot less enjoyable as a spectator sport by idiots shouting. Pretty much unwatchable in fact. A bit like tennis grunters. How dare they demand silence to serve and then grunt like a stuck porker. But back to golf. It was a lot more fun to watch before morons started shouting "Get in the hole," every time a player takes a putt. There seems to be a competition to see which imbecile can shout it first after the period of mandatory silence. Like posting "First" in the comments section of a blog post. As with a great deal of idiotic behaviour, when idiots see it for the first time, they think it's brilliant and join in. Now idiots can be heard shouting "get in the hole" after tee shots. I doubt it's ever been surveyed, but it's a good bet that almost every golf ball shouter is a person who also prays. And is of below average intelligence.

When children are scared, good parents comfort them and tell them stories to make them feel less scared and hopefully make them forget all about their fear. Although religions try to cash in the concept of good parenting by inappropriately using terms like father and child, they generally try to increase the sense of fear in their followers. They tell stories of hellfire and damnation and never ending torment and torture. Thanks, Father. Now I feel better. How much should I put in the collection plate to keep me safe?

Bad actors sense an opportunity to exploit normal, decent people by pretending to offer comfort when they are actually supplying more fear. You think things can get bad here on earth? I promise you, my religion has much worse in store for you if you don't get on your knees and give me your money. Eternal torture awaits you and the only way for you to avoid it is to come back here every Sunday and give me your money.

Superstition

Superstition is extremely common whether we really believe it or whether we just avoid walking under ladders because we're less likely to get covered in paint or hit by a falling hammer. Likewise, we try not to break mirrors because it makes a mess.

Sportsmen often have lucky underpants or lucky. They often have rituals to perform before an event although this may help them "getting into the zone".

Whether it's avoiding black cats or throwing spilt salt over your left shoulder, it's all just a load of old bollocks and a big waste of time and mental energy. Just ask Stevie -

> Very superstitious
> Writing's on the wall
> Very superstitious
> Ladder's 'bout to fall
>
> 13-month-old baby
> Broke the looking glass
> Seven years of bad luck
> The good things in your past
>
> When you believe in things
> That you don't understand
> Then you suffer
> Superstition ain't the way
>
> Stevie Wonder

The Paranormal

Another good way to waste time and energy is to believe in the paranormal. And/or the supernatural. Are they not the same thing? In terms of being bullshit, yes, of course they are.

But to aficionados, no they are not.

Paranormal is to Normal	as	Supernatural is to Natural
Paranormal is to Paralympic	as	Supernatural is to Supermodel
Paraglider is to Paratrooper	as	Supertrooper is to SuperMario
Paraplegic is to Paramedic	as	Panasonic is to Paralegal
Paleodiet is to Superman	as	Paradox is to Paracetamol

Hopefully, that clears that up.

Belief in the Paranormal and/or the Supernatural includes, but is not limited to belief in things such as ghosts, haunted houses, ghost trains, astrology, Halloween, spooky graveyards, pumpkin spice, fortune telling, talking to the dead, seances, reading tea leaves, reading coffee grinds, reading palms, reading psalms, reading Nostradamus, the Cosa Nostra, the Costa del Sol, Dos Equis and telling scary stories with an upward pointing flashlight held against the chin.

And exorcism. Which is, unbelievably, still a thing that some Catholic priests actually still do in the real world.

Modern day exorcisms often result in the death of the one with the alien in the belly. Talk about wacky. You couldn't make it up.

Acts of God

Acts of God are a staple of religion. They are the tales that convince people to devote their lives to their faith. A burning bush, a parting of the waters, a walking on water, a multiplication of loaves or a flood that covers the whole planet after selected animal couples journey impossible distances for the existential crisis cruise of a lifetime aboard Noah's Annihilation Princess.

But there is a major problem with such Acts of God. And that is that they are no more plausible than a Harry Potter adventure. There is not a single thing in any religion that could only be the work of a god. Something that could not possibly have just been made up by someone. Nothing that couldn't be fiction. Not a single thing.

So why are people so willing to believe not only that something is true, but that it is so amazing it could only be an act of a god? If it were possible to make up a story about an act of god, that, if it occurred, it would be impossible to dismiss as fiction, why has there never been a report of an act of god that could not be dismissed as fiction?

An argument could be advanced that that would apply to everything. But that's not the case. It would be possible to imagine any number of acts of god that could not be mistaken for anything else, but they are not part of any religion, because they've never happened.

An example -

On April 23, 2015, all the clocks on earth stopped. The sky changed from whatever it was, night, day, cloud, clear blue, to a glowing shade of red. The red sky tinged every part of the earth to shades of red, as though the earth were covered in a smoke haze at sunset, but there was no smoke. A sound boomed from above the clouds instructing everybody to go outside and look up. The instruction was delivered in a language that was miraculously understood by every individual, even though nobody on earth had ever heard it before.

Across the sky in big gold letters was written, "I am the one and only God. You must worship me. Further instructions will appear on your phones, iPads and computer screens, or on the walls of your place of residence if you don't have any electronic gizmos." If an English speaker was standing next to a Francophone and an Esperantist, they each believed they saw it all in their own language.

The first reaction was for people to look at each other to check that they were seeing what others were seeing. Many were suspicious that someone had slipped them a tab of acid or something stronger. Then came conversations with others to confirm they were experiencing the same thing and that thing was reality.

When people went to their screens they indeed found that God had left detailed instructions on how he should be worshipped. Even though everyone had seen it for themselves, the TV news all across the world was of nothing else. No pundit could offer any explanation other than it was the work of God.

Given that there are always a few idiots prepared to protest against anything no matter how much evidence exists, a few examples of lightning bolt direct hits and spontaneous combustion would remind people that a God who demands worship and never-ending praise also has no problem killing people, whether first born sons or almost everybody, if he's really pissed off.

Such an act of God would be undeniable. It would be the biggest event the world had ever seen. And it would never be questioned and never forgotten. It would also be well within the powers of an omnipotent god.

But no such event, or anything even one thousandth, one millionth, as potent or impressive as that has ever been reported. Ever.

And the reason offered for why an omnipotent god only ever behaves in an impotent manner is that he works in mysterious ways. Even though almost any human could think up much more impressive Acts of God than have ever been attributed to him, he's still looked on as being the almighty one.

The ability to fervently believe that implausible or utterly underwhelming events could only be the work of a god is yet another of the many failings of the poorly designed human brain.

Tribalism

A few thousand, or even a few hundred years ago, a warm affinity for the group of people who live in your district was not only comforting but also quite necessary, given that another tribe may be heading in your direction at any given moment. The other tribe may be randomly inbound for exploratory, accidental (they're lost) or nomadic purposes or they may have sent scouts ahead and are now en route to your tribe motivated by the eager anticipation of a spot of raping and pillaging.

One of the reasons it was useful to know and trust those in your tribe became very apparent in the melee of hand-to-hand mortal combat when the almost inevitable confrontation with another tribe kicked off. The reason that violence was almost inevitable was for the age-old reason that it only takes one nutter to start it, and there's always at least one nutter in every tribe. The village idiot is only a comic character when he's not also a dangerous psycho.

When facing a new opponent you might think, "Fuck, who's this? Uncle George, or some dirty old rapist that's about to kill me and do whatever while I'm still warm". And then cousin Billy would jump in and despatch the dirty old bastard and you'd still not be certain whether that was Uncle George or not but you'd be alive to fight the next round, knowing that cousin Billy was on your team. For whatever reason he may have in mind.

When tribalism was a useful self-defence tool people lived in relatively small areas, except for nomads who probably did a lot more fighting than tribes who preferred the comfort of a place called home. What nobody would have had any way of knowing back then was that tribalism would eventually turn out to be the opposite of a safety mechanism for most of humanity. Scientific advances in transportation meant we all effectively started living right next to each other in one place. The place we call planet Earth.

If you have one tribe living in a beautiful location, life can be almost blissful. (Apart from a wee bit of jealousy, lust, incest, abusive behaviour, dishonesty, or the nutter going off.) But when you have two tribes, they inevitably go to war. We are still many generations and many thousands of years from getting to grips with the idea that if we are going to make this globe a truly great place to live, we need to become one tribe. Regrettably, as discussed in the bit on intelligence, we're much too stupid for that to happen any time soon.

Evolution works very much slower than our communal brain advances in terms of technology. Orders of magnitude slower. And everything else is accelerating exponentially. If we're biologically tuned to a tribal attitude, it's going to take a lot of work to overcome it. The sort of work that isn't easy and isn't even understood by the mentally challenged.

Whilst tribalism is often praised for engendering a sense of belonging, community and social cohesion, these things all possess an inverse side which is the exclusion of others. The stronger the bonds inside the group, the greater the antipathy towards those outside the group. The most fanatical football fans enjoy bashing the fans of the opposing teams just as much as they enjoy getting drunk together. Or watching football. The most fanatical fans of some religions enjoy killing the fans of other religions so much that they take to the streets to celebrate the deaths of innocents belonging to other religions provided the death toll is high enough.

Tribalism, and especially religious tribalism, is one of the greatest dangers facing mankind from here on.

What makes tribalism so dangerous is that there are so many people who are prepared to advance their agendas by sowing division and encouraging intertribal hatred and slaughter, usually invoking a loving God as the architect of the carnage.

Tribalism can be the opposite of a group that looks after their own. When an individual loses faith in the tribe's behaviour or beliefs some tribes/cults take active steps to tear families apart.

Telling Lies

Lying is generally bad, and whilst mostly not ugly, it can be ugly sometimes. If a lie starts a war for example. CoughIraqcough.

Sometimes lying isn't bad. "Does my bum look big in this?" The kind, and therefore correct, lie used to be, "No, darling your ass looks as tight as a Brazilian beach volleyballer's butthole." Except you should've stopped talking before you got to hole. And butt. In fact, you should've probably left out the whole comparison thing and just said, "You look great." Now in the post-Kardashian era, "Hoo wee baby, from back here you look like a twerking hippo," is often the correct lie. Though not for everybody. Not every woman wants to look like she's carrying ready-to-sit-when-you-are wearable bean bags in the back of her bloomers.

Lying is a thing that humans learn early. Kids start lying to their parents from about the age of three.

Some parents fail to admonish their children straight away because early attempts at lying are so obvious and ludicrous that they're really cute. Parents are amused by the obvious lies and the child is encouraged to lie because the laughter is a reinforcing positive response.

If lying is not brought under control quickly enough, a child learns to lie as a way of getting what they want, sometimes in the belief that they are fooling the people they're talking to, but in the more serious cases, a kid discovers that he doesn't care if people know he's lying, as long as it still works to his advantage. When unchecked that can lead to a tendency towards sociopathy.

Such people can turn into pathological liars and even sociopathic dictators. Joseph Goebbels was an enthusiast of The Big Lie technique and encouraged his team to use it often and repeatedly. If your goal is to disrupt then tell the biggest lie possible. A lie told often enough becomes indistinguishable from the truth.

Becoming a habitual or pathological liar can lead to serious problems, both for the individual and everybody around them, often taking many years to fully manifest.

So why do some people become compulsive liars?

Compulsive lying is also known as pathological lying because its underlying causes may include personality disorders such as narcissistic personality disorder or antisocial personality disorder. People who crave attention or validation may be more likely to engage in compulsive lying as a way to get others to notice them. People with low self-esteem may engage in compulsive lying as a way to make themselves appear more interesting or successful to others.

Traumatic or abusive experiences in childhood may contribute to compulsive lying behaviour later in life as a way to cope with feelings of shame or insecurity. Some research suggests that compulsive lying may be related to certain neurological or cognitive factors, such as reduced grey matter in the prefrontal cortex or deficits in working memory.

Compulsive lying can be harmful to individuals and to those around them, as it can erode trust, damage relationships, and lead to legal or social consequences.

It's easy to say bullshit in a light-hearted manner to friends when you're not really calling them out over a direct lie but it's not easy to straight out accuse someone of lying to their face. And even harder if you don't know them or if they hold a position of power. Some people never get called out so they live in a bubble where lies become their norm. When a pathological liar attains a position of real power the consequences can be disastrous.

Humans are the only animals who lie so much. Most animals can't lie. Which is what makes the innocent facial expressions of surprised or confused dogs and cats so cute. Although many species can and do lie in order to have sex. Usually the male of the species. They inflate their chests or fan out their feathers to look larger and more powerful, or indulge in courtship dances.

Humans also dance during courtship. This is formalised at many weddings where the bride and groom lead off with their first dance as a married couple. It has been estimated that for 73% of married couples, their first dance is also their last dance, even if they remain married for decades.

The Both Sides Argument

The "both sides" argument is a favourite technique of malignant manipulators. It seems so innocent, so reasonable, to politely ask that both sides of an argument be given equal time and prominence. But it's only ever valid when both sides have equal or at least similar degrees of truth.

At a convention for interplanetary travel, for example, the Sherdingdon Flat Earth Society does not deserve equal billing, or an equal number of seats, on an expert panel alongside NASA or SpaceX. Likewise, the representatives of the Dunedin Underground Micro Biologists For Ultra Cool Knitwear Society have nothing of value to contribute to any conversation about vaccines.

Let's imagine two politicians being interviewed in a TV studio. The policy of one politician relies on the case that it's always raining and the other that it's always sunny. The liar, in this case, will insist that the reporter gives equal weight to his side of the argument, whereas the truth-teller will suggest that the reporter look out the window and tell the viewer whether or not it's raining.

Both sides of an argument are rarely of equal merit. Invoking the "both sides" schtick is invariably a deliberate attempt to plant misinformation. Giving equal prominence to a lie is not in any way providing balance. It always tips the scales in favour of the lie.

Drugs

Although drugs can be a lot of fun, there's no doubt that your life will be much better overall if you don't do them. Even moderate drug use can lead to impaired performance in many ways. But the worst thing about drugs is that we like them so much. And not only we humans. All manner of animals have discovered the joys of getting shit-faced.

When the New Zealand Tui (a native bird that can be identified by its patriotic All Black uniform with a fluffy, white, scrotal appendage dangling beneath its chin) discovers a flax bush with fermenting nectar they go at it like Scottish football fans, often ending up staggering about or passed out on the ground. Also famous for deliberately getting hammered are elephants, wallabies, monkeys and reindeer, who have such a fondness for magic mushrooms they've been observed fighting over them. Who knew they could be so human?

What sort of creator would design a brain that would crave a substance so much that people would fight and kill for it? A brain that even when cognisant of the dangers, will still ignore those dangers and continue to ingest the substance to the point of self-destruction. A brain so irrational, that even as I write these words I know I will have a drink or two tonight. (Rationale - it's Friday.) Drugs are bad, mkay?

There could also be an entry in the Ugly section for drugs,

not just because of the way people look after a five-year bender on methamphetamine, vodka, oxycontin, cocaine and the like, but because of the havoc that hard drugs inflict on everybody surrounding the addicts as well as on the addicts themselves. But that's not fun to dwell on, so we'll leave it here.

Lust

What are orgasms for? So that blondes know when to stop fucking.

That's a "joke", allegedly. The quotation marks are there to indicate that there was never a time when the alleged "joke" was actually funny.

The "joke" was apparently created by an incel. Incel is a portmanteau of involuntary celibate, a relatively recent term for (choose any four or more) angry, young, stupid, fat and ugly males, a subset of which is striving to find some respect by calling themselves Proud Boys. One of the many things this particular incel did not understand was that trying to crack wise about things you have no knowledge of, can often result in a self-own. The orgasm, as a sign that the show's over, an often perfect third-act finale that's unmatched anywhere in any other endeavour (and only occasionally involves a fat lady singing), applies not only to all humans, blonde, female, male and brunette, but to most animals on the planet, and is one of the few things we could award a creator maximum points for. If game shows for creators were a thing.

Hold on a second, if sex is so much fun, why is it in the bad section? Shouldn't it be categorised as good? As far as the body is concerned sex is definitely in the good section. But as for the brain?

Sex is well known for getting people into trouble. In fact of all the human desires, sexual lust is the thing that's most often the driving force behind calamities of one sort or another, from wrecking relationships, families, businesses, school committees, reputations and governments right up to starting wars. The Trojan War, for example, was named after a famous brand of condom because it was caused by insatiable lust.

The biological necessity of lust to ensure the reproduction of the species is a given, but is it correctly tuned so that we produce the right number of offspring? It has been said that men think about sex every seven seconds. Certainly, those of the Portnoy persuasion don't have much time to do anything but beat their meat, though most people manage to get a few other things done each day. A study was done to try to measure the number of sexy time thoughts people have each day but the results are a little vague for a variety of reasons. However, in the absence of a Neuralink thought tracker, they're the best we can do.

Men and women think about sex "several times" a day. For men, several means between eight and five hundred, and for women it means between seven and three hundred and fifty-two. Women are restricted to the number of babies they can carry during their fertile years, though a reasonable tally for those who are not members of religious cults is in the low single figures. The global average is 2.3.

According to Guinness World Records, "The greatest

officially recorded number of children born to one mother is 69, to the wife of Feodor Vassilyev (b. 1707–c .1782), a peasant from Shuya, Russia. In 27 confinements she gave birth to 16 pairs of twins, seven sets of triplets and four sets of quadruplets." What sort of confinements the poor woman was subjected to can only be imagined, but it should be noted that while her studly husband has his dates of existence recorded as well as his name, his poor wife, who did all the work, is not even afforded a name. Offeodor perhaps.

Let's assume that Offeodor was a woman who thought about sex less than the average twenty times per day and that her child-bearing years stretched for forty years. That would mean she thought about sex 292,000 times. The above-listed multiple births indicate that her 69 children came from 27 separate pregnancies, meaning that she thought about sex more than ten thousand times as often as was necessary. Although when she thought about sex she was probably praying for it not to happen.

The point of the above is to illustrate that the human race could easily survive with the lust knob turned down to about one. Or perhaps two, to add a level of redundancy. But a planet full of randy zombies marching around thinking about sex every time they see a bit of booty, and therefore not thinking about whatever productive thing they should be thinking about is not very intelligent design.

Procrastination

The reason that it took years longer to write this book than it should have - procrastination.

It's one of the most annoying afflictions to suffer from, and one of the hardest to overcome. I can't think of any reason why an intelligent designer would have even come up with the idea of the procrastination app for the human brain, let alone installed it in so many of us. Some say procrastination is just a fancy word for laziness but so what? The problem's the same.

You know that feeling of satisfaction you get from completing a task? Downing a cool lager as you survey a tidy garden with an immaculately mown lawn? The inner glow of a job well done? Rarer than a birthday for a procrastinator. Amcrastination would be bad enough.

Like addiction, you know what the problem is, but you can't control yourself sufficiently to overcome it. Because it is such an annoying thing, and because it is such an uncomfortable topic to research, I think I'll just put this section aside for now and come back to it later.

Self-Perception

How we think of ourselves is a huge topic. It fills many books. Deservedly so. It's complicated. It's also a bit dry for this book, so I'll try to give it a quick once-over. However it is important because how we think of ourselves determines how we behave.

A positive mental attitude can deliver positive results, while a negative attitude invites failure. We all know that. That's the simple version. How to maintain control over one's attitude is the difficult part. In all of human history, only one man has ever managed to maintain a constantly positive attitude throughout his lifetime. That was such an amazing achievement that they even made a movie about him. His name was Forrest Gump.

Self-knowledge, Self-image, Self-concept, Self-categorisation, Self-perception, Self-awareness, Self-reflection, Self-consciousness, Self-esteem, Self-assessment, Self-respect and Self-abuse are all connected concepts and yet each is worthy of its own discussion.

How many of us truly know what others think of us? Not many. Make that none. A public figure may have a better idea of that. Or not. For example, Donald Trump knows that millions of people idolise him and millions of people despise him. But does he know what those closest to him really think of him? Probably not.

We humans spend a lot of time worrying about how we appear to others, even if we pretend we don't. This is why we dress as we do, most of us conforming to the norms of our age group, while others deliberately dress counter to the norms, to demonstrate that they are different. One of the best things, perhaps one of the only good things, about growing older is that we care less about what others think of us. Thus older men can indulge their fondness for beige on beige.

It's not really surprising that we don't know what others think of us, as we can have erroneous perceptions of ourselves. Does my bum look big in this? If you have a big bum then probably, yeah. Even a big black sack may not be able to disguise a huge arse. A person suffering from anorexia nervosa can look in a mirror and think they look fat when they are, in reality, dangerously underweight. So we have no way of really knowing what we look like as far as others are concerned.

Even though we all do it to some extent, giving a shit about what strangers think of us is crazy. That should be obvious to us because although we may be judgemental of people we don't know, the thing is that we don't know them, and when they walk away we don't know, or care, where they're going, or why, or if we'll ever see them again, or what their name is, or what they do for living or anything. So our opinion of them has no value to them and is of no use to anybody. So why would some random stranger's opinion of me, matter to me?

And yet, our happiness depends on how we feel about

ourselves, which is affected by how we imagine others feel about us.

The amount of time humans, especially those of courtship age, spend on thinking about their appearance is not evidence of a well-designed brain.

Popularity and Fame

Wanting to be popular with people you know sounds a bit naff, but it's not a bad thing. Because if you're popular among people you know personally, it means there's a good chance that you're a pretty decent person. And that's why they like you. It means you'll likely have an enjoyable time whenever you see them. So be nice.

Being nice is a good start but it's not the only thing. Nice but boring will diminish your group of friends. Or at least diminish the quality of your friends if you enjoy laughing. Habitual pungent flatulence can also be a friendship destroyer. Halitosis won't beat nice and neither will flying phlegm or spittle. Funny or entertaining will help, but you'd have to be Ricky Gervais funny to outweigh any of the above-listed negatives. And even then, nah.

It's been said that there are only three reasons to bother maintaining relationships with other people. They either make you laugh, give you money or have sex with you. That sounds worse than it really is. If you broaden the topics, making you laugh can include any way that people entertain you, whether that involves actual laughter or perhaps a deep intellectual conversation, or going skydiving, or stamp collecting, or anything else that you find enjoyable, interesting or worthwhile. It doesn't include sitting in a cafe or bar for an hour or two being bored shitless by an old acquaintance with no sense of humour. Giving you money can include hanging out with people you work with, or for, or with people that may potentially, or actually, help you out in some way. And then there's sex. As always. Maybe it's as simple as whether you smile or frown when you see the caller ID.

A desire to be popular with a broad audience that you don't know personally is a different thing. People may desire admiration or adulation for a number of different reasons. Some people may feel a sense of insecurity or insignificance or unworthiness, and believe that fame will provide them with validation and self-worth. They might also hope that fame will endow them with power and importance. And sex. And lots of free stuff.

Being a kind, nice, decent person will not be enough to achieve widespread popularity. In fact, it probably doesn't matter at all, as there are any number of celebrities who have a reputation for being complete assholes and just a few that have a reputation for being wonderful people, like Dolly Parton, Shaquille O'Neal or Keanu Reeves.

One huge downside is when people do manage to gain instant fame by going viral. It's a bit like being a child star. Your chance of having continuing fame and adulation is almost non-existent. Then comes the crash. And the withdrawal symptoms. Even if it's just the disappearance of the fame, the pain can be intense. But if it comes with a backlash, a sudden piling on of millions of people declaring their hate for you, it can become unbearable. There's probably nothing more likely to lead to a lifetime of unhappiness than a few months of fame as a pretty, young Tik Tokker or Instagrammer.

For every person that achieves fame, there are millions who try but fail. Check out the auditions for TV talent shows for example. People who are prepared to risk humiliation for a chance to be a contender. Even the shows that concentrate on showcasing real talent versus humiliating the self-deluded can't resist dunking on some of the unfortunates.

To many people, a TV camera is like a candle to a moth. Even a one-second exposure on a big screen at a sporting event is enough to make most people so excited they jump up and down and wave like mad things. Why? Those of us watching at home have no idea who you are and we'll forget what you look like within seconds.

The same thing goes for people wanting to leave a legacy. Like having a road or a park or a park bench named after them. Take John Green Road for example. Who the fuck was John Green? Does anybody, apart from perhaps a relative, give a shit? Would anybody care if the road was named Grey Road instead? Who was Grey Road named after? Or is that just its colour? Who cares?

Even famous historical figures cease to mean anything much because we know them only as names and things that have been written about them. Not as real people. A lot of people know more about Indiana Jones than they do about Adolf Hitler.

Why is it that so many famous people have lives that end sadly or tragically? And not just the ones that deserve it.

Whilst being popular among friends, family and acquaintances is a positive thing, there's no real positive to the human brain's desire for fame. Given the degree to which many people are driven by it, and made miserable by either achieving it or their failure to achieve it, it's certainly not a good design feature.

Entitlement

I was born (and still identify as) a heterosexual male, into a white, middle-class family in a nice suburb of Auckland, New Zealand. A certain sector of the populace would deduce from that, that I probably have, and always will, behave like an entitled dickhead as a result. Sure there are times when I've behaved like a dickhead, but I don't remember behaving as though I was entitled to much. I've always felt lucky. Check out the first sentence. White, male, heterosexual, middle-class, urban New Zealand. That's a good hand to be dealt. A brilliant hand. It doesn't mean that white is better than any other colour, or that any of the other categories are better than their alternatives in any way, but every one of them does make life a little bit, or a lot, easier than being dealt one of their alternatives. Therefore lucky.

That was a hard paragraph to write without sounding arrogant, but I hope I made the point that being lucky does not mean being better.

In 2021 I had a bit of luck in terms of the price of bitcoin rising and making me a little bit richer (or a little bit less poor, depending on the wealth of the observer) than I had been the day before. At the supermarket I decided to buy some food that was a bit more gourmet and therefore expensive than usual because my inner voice said, "You deserve it." Which made me instantly recoil.

Deserve it? No, I didn't. I got lucky. Simply having enough money to invest a small amount was lucky in itself. Sure it was my decision to buy bitcoin rather than Nikola shares, so I deserved a little bit more credit than if I'd bought an expired lottery ticket, but not much. Not enough to make me feel entitled to anything. To deserve anything special. I hadn't even done so much as help an old lady across a road. I'd just got lucky. Again.

It's amazing how a small windfall can make you believe you are more worthy. Deserving. Entitled. So it's not surprising that those born into very lucky circumstances feel that they deserve all the good things that come their way. It's not so much that their brains have been dissolved by their wealth, it's that all of our brains work that way. (This is not a get-out-of-jail-free card. Your childhood is not an excuse for shitty behaviour. If you're a serial killer or a rapist, fuck you, go to jail.)

Entitlement, when observed in the wild, even in brief interactions, perhaps being rude or deliberately demeaning to a waiter or shop assistant, is the common human trait that makes me most often want to punch someone in the face. If I was big and tough enough, perhaps I'd feel sufficiently entitled to do so.

THE UGLY

The worst aspects of the human brain are truly ugly. Although it's a very unpleasant thought, some human beings have such a lack of empathy that they can kill, steal, lie and torture without any sense of guilt or remorse. They reside in the penthouse of the psychopath pyramid. Specialists in the field of psychopathy estimate that they may comprise up to about 1% of the general population. Which doesn't seem like all that many until you realise that you live within walking distance of a few hundred people. Or a few thousand. And psychopaths know how to drive cars and catch buses.

Fortunately, most psychopaths are not so crazy that they don't care about themselves. So they care about the consequences of killing the next door neighbour for playing loud music, though they'd be happy to do so if they thought they could get away with it. If your pets start dying it might be time to turn down the music. Or better still, move.

Unfortunately, it's not only psychopaths who commit the worst atrocities. Lots of seemingly normal people (mostly men) can be coerced into committing the most horrific acts of savagery. On many occasions throughout history, leaders of personality and/or religious cults have unleashed their brainwashed followers to initiate an orgy of violence, genocide, torture, mutilation and sexual assault in the name of terrorism or their chosen god, usually both.

Even without the brainwashing, merely being cast into a theatre of war can be enough to transform outwardly normal men into killing machines. It's safe to say that not many of the participants of the My Lai Massacre were psychopaths when they left the USA, though lots of them were no longer normal on their return. The scary thing about situations like that is it only takes one psycho to start the ball rolling. Like the guy in the pub in Glasgow who throws the first punch.

Human trafficking, sexual slavery, rape, child abuse and the like are all too common whether carried out for financial gain or to satisfy personal depravity.

It's often pointed out how irrational it is to claim the existence of an omniscient, loving god when the world is full of starvation, disease and deprivation. The same thought can be applied when considering the most evil qualities of the human brain.

Would a designer who was not evil include such evil in the design of the human brain?

Violence

Lots of people are not violent. They never hit anyone or anything. Yay. If only…

Lots of people are occasionally violent. They rarely hit anyone or anything, but may be driven to lash out and punch a hole in a wall or door, or smash a mirror. Or even wreck a whole room, tipping over shelves, bookcases, smashing paintings and the like. Especially if they're a character in a TV drama. It occurred to me that I've not, in real life, ever seen anyone smash things against a wall. In anger that is. But of course, it's pretty unusual for anyone else to be there when the protagonist gets the news that makes him go bananas.

Quite a lot of people (mostly men) are often violent. Which is far too often. They're violent because they're angry with the world and full of resentment for some real or imagined reasons which makes them capable of exploding into violent rage with little or no provocation. Or they're violent because they enjoy fighting. As seen in all of the "rougher" pubs in any town on earth, and most football stadiums in Europe. Notably the Den, the home of Millwall FC on the Isle of Dogs in London. According to Wikipedia, "The stigma of violence attached to Millwall can be traced back over 110 years."

Perhaps after a week of working a shitty low paying job, the weekend provides the opportunity for a wild, head-clearing blowout. As Bernie Taupin wrote for Elton John -

It's getting late, have you seen my mates?
Ma, tell me when the boys get here
It's seven o'clock, and I wanna rock
Want to get a belly full of beer

Oh, don't give us none of your aggravation
We had it with your discipline
Oh, Saturday night's alright for fighting
Get a little action in

But whatever the excuse or reason, whether valid or not, why would a benevolent designer program any human brain to have a predisposition to violence?

The Violence Industry

Humans love to watch other humans beat the shit out of each other.

This is why we are absolutely hopeless at creating societies that are good to live in. Lots of us, plus or minus some amount, have little empathy for other humans.

Or at least for humans that aren't family, or the same colour, or the same socio economic tribe. Or for lots of other reasons used as an excuse to dismiss the idea of feeling any concern for them. This is the reason that conservative and libertarian political parties have the viability that they do. Many of us are fucking arseholes.

The Romans used to love to watch Christians being torn apart by lions. (Something they did before the smart ones realised that the real money was in the bullshit the Christians were selling.)

Muslims are often seen in clips on social media gathering to whoop and cheer whilst enjoying the suffering of those who violate Sharia law, whether gays being thrown off roof tops, or women being stoned to death or flogged in a public square for indulging in the pleasures of the flesh their god blessed them with and then forbade them from.

But back to the Romans. Howling, bloodthirsty fans filled arenas to watch vicious fights to the death between unwilling participants. Of course that was before we became too civilised to enjoy such things. Things such as cage fights. One day somebody realised that putting a couple of angry humans in a cage and paying them to beat the shit out of each other wasn't illegal. What? Most people kind of thought it must have been because it was so barbaric, but no. That's what lawyers are for. Sign some contracts. Smash some heads in. All good. Let the money roll.

The crowds are huge. The pay-per-view rakes in billions. We are an ugly, horrible, shit stain of a species.

An alligator may spontaneously tear the leg off another alligator for no apparent reason (apart from the stress of being held in captivity), and humans will enjoy watching that, but human on human violence is even more satisfying. Humans salivate at the prospect of getting dressed up to go to a stadium to watch desperate humans beat the consciousness out of other desperate humans.

Desperate may mean desperate for money (for beginners), or desperate for adulation (for stars). It's hard to imagine any but those who are desperate in some way signing on to the possibility of having some horrible, sweaty animal sit on their chest and punch the shit out of their head until they've suffered brain damage.

Brain damage doesn't matter to the viewers. They've paid their money, they'll have their blood.

If the human brain is the design of an all-knowing, all-caring, all-loving god, what the fuck is that all about?

Sure the animal instinct of fight vs flight makes sense, but to enjoy the sight of one of your peers getting beaten or butchered... That's not good.

Rape

It doesn't take much in the way of imagination to understand that rape, especially when exacerbated with violence, is likely to destroy the life of the victim. Or at least destroy their feeling of freedom and severely curtail the ability to pursue happiness.

Yet whoever wrote the Ten Commandments did not think it made the cut of the top ten rules to obey. Unlike murder. Or honouring your father and mother. Or being jealous of your neighbour's ass. Is that why so many men are rapists? Because the Bible doesn't think it's so bad?

According to the Bible if a man rapes a virgin he has to "give her father fifty shekels of silver, and she shall become his wife because he has violated her; he cannot divorce her all his days." Deuteronomy 22:28-29

Fifty shekels. And she shall become his wife. That's a hell of a deal for a victim of rape. What a caring and loving God. There are some states in the USA that still use such passages as guidance in their statutes.

The Bible also says that a man who rapes a married woman shall be put to death. Why the different outcomes? Because a married woman is another man's property, and the crime in that case is against a man which is much more serious.

It's a horrible topic so let's not dwell on it longer than to say whoever might have designed a human brain with such a high incidence of rapey behaviour built in was neither an intelligent nor a moral designer.

Slavery

Slavery used to be fine. The men in charge of things said so. The men in charge of things, or high net worth individuals as they're known in certain circles these days, have always been looked up to and respected. Or at least feared. Those in charge of things have always known that there's no better way to become a wealthy individual than to have a large workforce that requires only food and lodging in return for long days of hard work.

Slavery has been perfectly acceptable throughout almost all of human history, only beginning to go out of fashion very recently, in the 19th century. It continues in many places, and perhaps in every country if you count sweat shops and brothels. I'm not claiming that all sewing machine operators and sex workers are slaves, but a lot of them are.

The constant struggle over unionisation, workers' rights and the minimum wage illustrates the ongoing efforts of rich men trying to exploit a labour force for the absolute minimum possible outlay.

So how does slavery qualify for the Ugly part of the book after being so widely accepted and utilised for so long? If it's not obvious to you, then you have a deficient imagination or at least one very ugly area in your brain. Unfortunately you're not in the minority, at least historically.

Even the "good book" seemed to think that slavery was okay. There are passages that deal with the treatment of slaves (eg Exodus 21:21), but there is no statement to the effect that slavery is wrong.

So it's unsurprising that the design of the human brain should be deficient in this area.

Terrorism

The idea of attacking unsuspecting civilians in order to advance your personal, political or religious agenda is abhorrent, whether it's crashing planes, blowing things up, driving trucks through crowds or firing guns.

Any brain that thinks it's fine to kill or maim people who may have never even been aware of what your problem is, is very unintelligently designed.

Bigotry

It's pretty much self-evident that bigotry is a design fault. At least it is, if you're not a bigot. If you are a bigot I really don't care what you think, because bigotry is ugly and bigotry is always counter-productive, at best.

It's hard to think of a reason that an intelligent designer would create different races and then create inter-racial hatred, but here we are. Humans. We have bad brains. We can think up all sorts of stupid shit to justify all sorts of bad behaviour.

It's pretty unusual to see any diversity amongst birds on a wire, but it's also unusual to see flocks of birds at war with one another. They all just get on with what they're doing. They respect each other's boundaries and territories and get on with doing their own stuff. Unless of course, one of them looks like food to another one, but that's a whole different thing.

Bird species do not reproduce with one another. That might explain the whole bird on a wire thing. Meaning the habit birds have for sitting in a line with their own kind, although if occasionally a different bird happens to pop in, or just be there when the others arrive, it's usually not a deal. Certainly not a big deal. Different species. No sexual attraction. No natural animosity.

But humans of all races do reproduce with one another. Same species. Different branches. Now often to be found sitting on the same branches. Which makes some feel uncomfortable.

Bigotry is just a way for low quality humans to imagine that they are superior to other humans. Humans that they know very little about. If it were just a case of sitting on a different wire it wouldn't be a big deal, but it gets much uglier than that. Much, much uglier. Genocide ugly. And that's as ugly as ugly gets.

Hypocrisy

Hypocrisy is the ugly quality that allows dishonest people to hold positions of authority and trust based on the lies they tell about themselves. Disappointingly, it's so commonplace, especially amongst politicians and preachers that many, perhaps a majority, of those who we entrust with the wellbeing of our societies are often totally untrustworthy.

Hypocrisy is the icing on the lie that elevates it from bad to ugly.

Ugly - A sanctimonious religious organisation that has been routinely raping children on a massive scale for hundreds of years. Hypocrites. Ugly hypocrites.

Also ugly, really, really ugly, but not quite as ugly as the above - Non-sanctimonious pedophiles affiliated to NAMBLA (North American Man Boy Love Association) who routinely rape children. At least we know who they are, which should make them easier to catch and lock up.

Ugly - A sanctimonious megachurch preacher who uses tax-free religious donations to pay a pool boy to have sex with his wife while he watches. Hypocrite.

Ugly - A sanctimonious, fervently anti-gay senator who is

outed enjoying a glory hole in an airport toilet. Anyone who makes it a part of his day job to target and criminalise and destroy the lives of a group of people that he pretends he is not a part of, is really just scum. Hypocrisy of the worst kind.

Not ugly and not even bad - An openly gay senator who does not lie about his sexual preferences.

Ugly - A supreme court judge who professes an unimpeachable moral code and standard of ethics who takes "gifts" from wealthy "friends".

False Witness

The bloke that wrote the Ten Commandments decided that bearing false witness was one of the big ten. While it might not seem quite as worthy as that given the notable absences of some fairly important things, it is in fact a pretty big deal.

Nothing spreads faster than a malicious lie. The juicier the better. And once spread, nothing is harder to completely erase than a malicious lie.

Which is one of the things that makes "just asking questions" such a vile trick to indulge in. "Is it true that Congressman Barbrady was charged with raping four infant children but after being granted name suppression he then got off on a technicality? I don't know. But some people are saying it's true. At least they will be by the time they hear this story from their neighbour. I'm not saying it's true. Just asking the question, but you know what they say, there's no smoke without fire. I'm just asking. Is there any smoke? I don't know." Congressman Barbrady may have never even thought about abusing a child but that doesn't mean the stink won't stick. Especially if allies of the slanderer get serious about using the persistent repetition trick in order to establish the truth of the lie.

We've all heard the "one lousy goat" joke, but the truth it contains is that even if the character in the joke had never mounted a single goat, sheep, chicken, pig or anything else in field or farmyard, the dirt on his reputation was as indelible as the blood on Lady Macbeth's hands. Bearing false witness is, among lies, a special level of heinous as it has the potential to destroy the whole life of someone falsely accused.

Spreading lies about others is a trick often perpetrated by children when they've been caught in bad behaviour. But just because something is childish and simplistic, doesn't mean that it's easy to combat. There's no easy way to counter a small child who repeatedly asks "Why?" to everything you say. Or repeats your words back to you. Even worse is that such annoying games might go on forever because of the rule that says you can't punch small children in the face no matter how annoying they are.

We seem to be entering an era of ever more corrupt politicians but is that really what's happening? It used to be that when a senator was discovered taking bribes or whatever, they were called out. The new game is far more deceitful. It's where a politician accuses his opponents of crimes that he himself is about to commit, so that when his own criminality comes to light he can claim that his opponents are just saying that to get back at him because he already accused them of the same things.

What vile personality would do such things? Clearly an example of unintelligent design.

Corruption

The thing that makes corruption such a perennial favourite of those with no moral standards is that the returns are better than anything else imaginable.

A gift of a first class holiday may result in a return of millions. A luxury RV could buy a favourable court ruling. An open-ended, cost-plus contract to supply a branch of the military may be worth billions in profit to the lucky recipient and may have only cost a million or two in donations to a SuperPAC.

Any criminal in the habit of doing a risk/reward analysis before deciding on which bank or pharmacy to rob would not believe the numbers. Why are these deals so wildly disproportionate? It's because the person receiving the bribe is providing the payback out of someone else's money. They don't give a shit that the return is massive because, regardless of how big it is, it doesn't cost them anything. Unless they get caught.

For the fat cats dishing out the bribes, the risk is minimal. There's nothing illegal about making a donation to a political campaign. Even when the system is so obviously rotten there's almost no chance of fixing it, because the pig's back is so vast, with so many people on it, it's like trying to change the course of a supertanker with a toy tugboat.

Thieves, scammers and hackers

The low value, non-violent family of crimes known as misdemeanours may not involve much in the way of poorly considered neural design. The causes may be more environmental than biological. It would be hard to live in a community where petty theft was the norm and remain completely unaffected by the fact that you're the only one without a bag of candy.

Demeanour means the way one deports oneself. A misdemeanour, therefore is a misstep in that deportment. A misstep is not even as serious a stubbed toe. Although there's nothing non-serious about the type of stubbed toe often suffered by young New Zealanders running too fast in jandals, when they flip the full face of the big toe open to the breeze. Ouch.

Examples of petty larceny almost made the bad section as opposed to the ugly section, on account of being petty, but the bad section of traits of the human brain is mostly dealing with afflictions that harm only the sufferer as opposed to other people.

The other thing that places petty larceny at the bottom end of the ugly scale is that humanity may actually need it. Would life be too perfect and therefore boring without it? Who knows. But we've all heard the stories about perfect little communities where nobody locks their doors and then one day the village weirdo's brain goes haywire and he turns into the nation's most celebrated psycho killer.

Brainwashing and Misinformation

Throughout history some humans have always strived for control over other humans. There are various ways to achieve control, such as the employer/employee relationship, the owner/slave relationship, and the devout Christian or Muslim husband/wife relationship. Most parents try to control their children right up to the time they discover they are no longer able to.

Politicians need to control their party members and their core supporters. To maintain control they tell their followers what they imagine their followers want to hear. When they stuff up and say the wrong thing they scramble to try to pretend they meant something else and they say new things designed to keep their minions in line.

A totally honest politician would never succeed. Which raises the distasteful truth that telling lies is part of a politician's job. As a result, the world revolves on disinformation and misinformation. Which is in turn made many times worse by politicians that lie deliberately and maliciously, rather than out of necessary expedience.

Deliberately lying to the public is shameful, but it becomes downright evil when the lies are directed at enemies or minorities with the aim of sowing discontent and seeding violence. The repetition of lies becomes propaganda and brainwashing.

Maintaining control of a religious congregation involves insisting that they attend services at least once a week. This has the effect of reinforcing the myth, so that it becomes embedded and accepted as fact, as well as maintaining the income flow. When people stop attending church their faith inevitably fades over time, until one day they realise that they no longer believe.

Interestingly there's never been (as far as I know) a class action lawsuit of ex-church members demanding their money back because it was taken from them under false pretences. Could it be framed in a way that made it incumbent on the church to prove they were telling the truth about heaven and the afterlife?

Church elders long ago realised that indoctrinating the fresh, impressionable minds of children was the best way to develop and maintain a subservient flock. But is it a benign way to impart the teachings of an all loving God, or is it a cynical attempt to brainwash them to keep them in the fold? Is it in fact a form of child abuse? Yes. Yes it is. Of course it is.

Child Abuse

Child Abuse is about as depressing and sad and odious as a topic can get, so I'll try to keep it brief.

Children are abused by adults in a number of ways, from neglect, to assault, to sexual abuse, to mental abuse. Each requires a slightly different design fault in the cranial programming of the adults involved.

Lots of children are subject to neglect, starvation and physical assault because their parents or caregivers are drug addicts. Which is not an excuse, but their inability to look after themselves does at least explain why they're incapable of looking after a child. Some parents are incapable of looking after children whether or not they have substance abuse problems because of personality disorders or some other mental deficiencies. Whilst not as egregious as those parents who deliberately mistreat their children, the effect on the children is still appalling.

Children are also subject to abuse outside their homes, most commonly in schools run by churches and in churches themselves. The Catholic Church may be one of the worst offenders, but the problem is endemic throughout all religions. If you place defenceless children in the custody of unmarried men with no oversight what do you think might happen? What sort of men might be attracted to a job that requires them to have no sexual contact with other adults, but gives them unfettered access to children? As a bonus that job comes with membership of an organisation that protects its brethren whenever they are discovered committing their vile deeds. Why would non-pedophiles be interested in those jobs? The mass rape of children is not a by-product of such a situation, it is the only possible outcome.

The best argument that can be made for the treatment of children by churches is that all they were trying to do was brainwash the children into fearing God for the rest of their lives. And that the institutionalised mass rape of children was merely collateral damage.

Sexual abuse of children also occurs outside such institutions. In recent times it's become disturbingly apparent that it's a fair bit more common than previously thought. Sexual attraction is a necessary feature of the human brain, but sexual desire that veers off into such depravity that it can only be satisfied by raping and permanently damaging children, would be a design blunder of the highest order. And if not a blunder, that just makes it worse.

Because this book is about God and the human brain it makes sense to focus on God's involvement in the abuse of children, since God, as the creation scientists would have it, is responsible for programming the brains of the adult human abusers here on earth. God recommends the beating of children -

Whoever spares the rod hates their children, but the one who loves their children is careful to discipline them.

Proverbs 13:24

I guess loving parents need to be careful not to love them too much.

When viewed objectively, it becomes head smashingly obvious that religion is just bullshit made up by some very dishonest people, so why do so many humans would fall for it? Because they were told the big lie about God and had that lie repeated to them over and over throughout their whole childhood. Without the indoctrination of children, religion really wouldn't stand a chance.

Lunatics such as Kenneth Copeland and Joel Osteen routinely scream at their congregations about the "Fear of God" as something to be admired. Children are already afraid of the dark and what may be under the bed, but on top of that good God fearing Christian parents tell them that there's a ghostly creature who's always there, right beside them, who can read their minds and who will send them to eternal damnation if they so much as think dirty thoughts. What? Why tell such nasty things? Why escalate their fears? How is using propaganda to establish and reinforce belief in a massive lie a good thing?

We reserve the word terrorist for arguably the most despised category of human, yet deliberately instilling terror in the fragile, impressionable brains of your own children is somehow not terrorism?

Millions of humans routinely perpetrate the mental abuse of children, making them fear God, telling them they're subject to the wrath of God if they so much as think bad thoughts. What the fuck is wrong with these assholes? Why would you want to mentally torture your own children? For fuck's sake, even if you think it's true, shouldn't a loving parent shield their child from such mental terror? At least until they're old enough to deal with it. Perhaps until they're about 45 or so.

Most animals try to teach their offspring about the reality of the world they live in, to help them thrive and survive, yet some humans choose to brainwash their children to live in a state of constant fear and believe in things that have nothing to do with reality.

For their own protection children are not permitted in casinos, brothels, bars, sex shops and the like. They're not allowed to drive cars, or own guns, or smoke cigarettes, or operate dangerous machinery. Yet it is absolutely fine for them to be taken into large, scary, magical buildings where they're told that they are sinners and therefore are at serious risk of being burnt alive. They're told that there is a judgemental God who can see everything they do, and even know exactly what they're thinking. And right now they're in his house, a house so big and scary that it makes the gingerbread house look like a gingerbread house. I can't think of many things more damaging to a kid who'd rather just go out and play in the sunshine

Whilst the brainwashing of children may not be as harmful as physical and sexual abuse as far as the individual children are concerned (just ignoring for a moment that they often occur together), the damage to society at large is devastating. A society of misinformed zombies living their lives based on lies is an unforgivable waste of the human potential that nature bestowed on us.

I've been told that I shouldn't be too critical of religion because our society and our culture is based on it. To which I respond that the traditional societies and cultures of some parts of the world, from Africa to Asia, have been almost totally erased by an imported Arab religion that now controls them. Also, the problem with basing anything on something that's not true will eventually lead to its failure. If you were to construct a building or a city based on a geological report provided by somebody who just made it up, you shouldn't be surprised if your city collapses into a sink hole after a heavy rainfall. Likewise you shouldn't be surprised if the wings fall off an aircraft that was built using fraudulently certified aluminium. There are thousands of gods who are no longer believed in. The societies who believed in them are also long gone.

Pseudoscience

Where to begin? The thing that makes pseudoscience ugly, rather than just stupid, is that for it to exist, some dishonest asshole had to make it up. And then tell everyone that the bullshit they just made up is true. This should be self evident, but just in case... Science is the observation of the physical world around us with an attempt to measure, understand and explain how it all works. Pseudoscience is just bullshit that some asshole made up. And then a whole lot of people were deceived to believe. Sort of like religion.

The most dangerous thing about pseudoscience is that many people try to treat serious illnesses with pseudo-medicines such as naturopathic solutions, aka water. So it's not only a lie, it's a dangerous lie that often ends in heartbreak.

I thought it might be useful to have a look at a few of the topics in the field, so I hit Wikipedia for a "List of topics characterised as pseudoscience." The list of headings alone, without following the links to the pages of actual info, or misinfo, seems to number in the thousands. Therefore TL;DR. I couldn't be arsed even trying to count them.

I did notice one of the headings was for something called Water Memory. "Water memory is the purported ability of water to retain a memory of substances previously dissolved in it even after an arbitrary number of serial dilutions. It has been claimed to be a mechanism by which homeopathic remedies work, even when they are diluted to the point that no molecule of the original substance remains, but there is no evidence for it."

I like the line, "but there is no evidence for it." How the hell could there be? How the hell would you even ask water what it remembered? I can't remember what was dissolved in me yesterday but at least I can communicate that. Hey, water. Would you mind answering a few questions just for the record?

So there are two problems with the brains of people involved with pseudoscience - those who make it up and those who accept it.

The rise of pseudoscience has coincided with a decrease in public trust of science. I almost wrote real science, but science needs no adjective. Something is either scientific or not. If a drug has not been tested using scientific methods, it should not be taken. Orally or seriously.

People who are ignorant of what science is, are nevertheless happy to express strident opinions on things they have absolutely no knowledge of, let alone expertise in. Before anti-vaxxers, there were antivaccinationists, who hired a New York ad agency re-brand them before re-entering the battle with ideas and sentiments that were basically the same as their ignorant predecessors of years gone by.

Antivaccinationists were mostly against laws requiring immunisations. They were for freedom. Freedom over their own bodies and freedom from state-mandated vaccinations.

When a smallpox outbreak in the US in the 1870s led to a call for vaccination campaigns, at least two Anti-Vaccine Leagues were started in response. They argued through local and Supreme courts for the right to stay un-vaccinated. Fortunately they lost and smallpox was eventually eradicated.

Whether smallpox will remain eradicated remains to be seen, although before placing any bets on that a viewing of the movie Idiocracy is recommended.

Environmental Vandalism

Actions that deliberately harm the environment, thereby disregarding the well-being of future generations, are morally indefensible.

It's hard to say which is worse, a multi-billion dollar oil company that establishes, by means of its own research, that its core business model will almost certainly lead to the ruination of the environment via climate change, or the redneck who modifies his climb-up-a-ladder-to-get-in truuuuck with truck nuts and ridiculously large wheels, to "roll coal", in other words cause it to blow massive clouds of carcinogenic black smoke, for the perverse enjoyment of "owning the libtards".

Actually no. It's not hard. The redneck with the truuuck is just stupid. He can't help being stupid and nobody can fix stupid. The oil company executives are not stupid. They've made a calculation that it's more important for them to have holidays on superyachts than it is to try to maintain the planet as a place for humanity to survive.

Although they never get actual blood on their hands, they may be part of the team that causes our extinction. Assholes.

Malignant Narcissism

Narcissism, as discussed earlier in the segment about traits that are merely bad, is a recognised personality disorder.

Whilst unpleasant, milder grades of narcissism are fairly common and nowhere near as bad as things can be on that spectrum. Self-esteem could be seen as mild narcissism or healthy narcissism, but the further the knob is cranked up the scale, the uglier it becomes. Filling the gap between narcissists and sociopaths are malignant narcissists. Malignant narcissists care only about themselves and think only about themselves. They can take offence at any tiny perceived criticism, and may hold a grudge for a very long time, perhaps for their whole life.

They are so focussed on being perceived as the best, the smartest, the best-dressed, the best looking, the richest, the most powerful, that they will go to sometimes comical lengths to try to make that happen. One or two trips to the plastic surgery may be understandable, but when we see someone who's obviously had twenty attempts at facial rejuvenation it's hard not to feel pity, even though it's entirely their own fault. Or at least the fault of their personality disorder.

If their target is power and wealth however, the victim list grows. If they control a company, their employees will suffer, especially those who work most closely with them. If they control a country, everybody will suffer.

About 6% of the general population exhibit signs of pathological narcissism. This number rises among those in positions of power or authority.

The hardest part about trying to deal with narcissists is that their very condition means that they see themselves as outstanding and there's no possible way that there could be anything wrong with them. And the more narcissistic they are, the more ridiculous their self perception becomes.

Designing such a glaring fault into the human brain, a fault that always brings unhappiness or worse to all those around the sufferer would be bad enough, but then to make it unfixable because of its own inbuilt Catch-22? That's just depraved.

Psychopaths and Sociopaths

If you suspect that your next door neighbour is a psychopath, start looking for somewhere else to live. If you suspect your next door neighbour is a sociopath, start looking for somewhere else to live. If your neighbour's kid starts pulling the wings off flies and torturing puppies, start looking for somewhere else to live.

Anyone who saw The Silence of the Lambs has no trouble remembering the character of Hannibal Lecter, a classic, prototypical, full-blown psychopath. As terrifying as he may have been, he was at least fictional. Ted Bundy was real. And so was Jeffrey Dahmer. Both were serial killers. Bundy sexually abused his victims while Dahmer ate his. Were they psychopaths or sociopaths or both?

The American Psychiatric Association doesn't draw a defining line between psychopaths and sociopaths. Instead it puts them both in a bucket labeled Antisocial Personality Disorder. But that's wimping out somewhat. So I'll offer a definition.

Psychopaths are more cunning. They'll smile pleasantly while planning to dismember you. Sociopaths are more pathological against society as a whole. They'll not only throw empty bottles out the car window, they'll aim them at oncoming cars or pedestrians. They have so little respect for anybody around them that they won't bother to try to hide their disdain for you. They'll push you out of the way to get through a doorway, whereas a psychopath will remember that you didn't get out of his way and he'll kill you for it later. The sociopath will cause as much damage or injury as he feels like doing, but it's unlikely to make him happy. Whereas a psychopath enjoys subjecting others to horrific pain. He'll look forward to it, get off on it, probably sexually, and he'll enjoy reminiscing about it afterwards. That's why he'll keep souvenirs and revisit the crime scene, something a sociopath is less likely to bother with because he'll have moved on and be busy causing mayhem elsewhere.

So there's a line between them for what it's worth. Both of them are as beneficial as cancer and it becomes more and more important for humanity to find an effective way to identify and remove them from the normal population. Because if humanity is extinguished by our own hand, something that has been a real possibility for many years now, it will be someone from the O'path family that does it.

It's pretty much self-evident that an intelligent designer would only install the psycho app into the human brain if he was an asshole.

But wait. Not all psychopaths and sociopaths murder people, or even wreak havoc and destruction wherever they go. In fact quite a few psychopaths are "respectable" business leaders or politicians. And that's an even bigger problem. It's pretty much a sure thing that a psychopath is also a malignant narcissist. Empathy doesn't ride along well with serial killing.

Anything that a psychopath will achieve in the world of business or politics will only ever be to the benefit of the psychopath, because that's all he cares about.

Which brings us to demagogues and despots.

Demagogues and Despots

Like psychopaths and sociopaths, demagogues and despots have similarities and differences.

Similarities. One. None of them are going to win any Mr Niceguy competition. Correction. Noone else is going to win any Mr Niceguy competition in any despot's country. Two. The world would be a better place without them. Any of them. At all.

Differences. Demagogues might still conform with some of the principles of democracy. Or at least pretend to. Despots often rise to power from within a democracy, but they will quickly remove all limits to their power and will use police and armed forces to maintain control often with brutal displays of power in order to suppress any dissent.

Demagogues may transform into despots, but despots don't go back. And they don't go away. Until they die. Sometimes violently.

The playbook for creating a population that will succumb to eventual despotism is well known, and has been brilliantly illustrated by writers such as George Orwell. But that make us no less likely to become victim to it.

A strongman leader needs an enemy to be strong against. If the country has no genuine enemy, a strongman will create one. He'll tell the people that the enemy is coming for them, coming for their jobs, coming for their women, coming for their country. Give the people an enemy to fear, an enemy to hate. Tell them scary stories. The scarier the better. The less truthful the better. Tell people their way of life is under threat and only the strongman can save them. Why not? People can't tell shit from Shinola. When fact-checked, claim the fact checkers are also the enemy. Demonise the free press. Destroy any possibility of a national conversation in which facts matter. Destroy the very foundation of facts and truth.

Without truth, without facts, a decent society cannot exist.

Without demagogues and despots, a decent society would become the default position.

Despots

The history of humanity could also be called the history of absolute bastard psychopaths in positions of power. If you tried to tell a sanitised version of history by removing all the nasty, sadistic, mentally deranged, professional serial killers, you would fail miserably. There'd be more blank pages than stories.

By way of illustration, here are some very brief outlines of some of the worst bastards who ever lived.

Attila tha Killa the Hun was a terrific name for a psychopath. Like a boy named Sue, Attila tha Killa the Hun's destiny was almost set by it. Attila rose to power in 434 AD in the best possible way for a genocidal maniac, by killing his brother. Attila's excuse was that he had heard his brother was starring in a travelling pornography circus using the stage name Attila the Hung, although there's no reason to think that story is anything other than complete bullshit. After killing his brother, Attila dropped "tha Killa" from his name as he'd heard rumours that people were calling him Attila tha brotha Killa the Hun. He also went on a mass killing spree so as to divert attention from the incident involving his brother.

Just in case people didn't appreciate the full measure of his nastiness, Attila purportedly said, "There, where I have passed, the grass will never grow again." That story seems a lot more plausible, but then again, how would you know?

Although his rise to power occurred in what is now called Hungary, it was not named because of any famine caused by Attila's scorched earth behaviour during his reign of 19 years. In the mid 20th century the German army was nicknamed the Hun when it started to emulate Attila's activities, though possibly not for that reason.

Genghis Khan incited the Mongol hordes to brutally slaughter their way through a huge part of Central Asia and China for 20 years from 1206. It is unclear (to me at least) exactly what motivated him to do this, although it was generally expected of ruthless bastard leaders of the time to do such things. A tally of a few thousand would have probably sufficed, but Genghis Khan's piles of tens of millions of dead bodies was an absolutely stellar effort and cemented him for all time as one of humanity's greatest ever psychopaths.

Timur, who reigned for 35 years (1370-1405), was undefeated as a military commander and is widely regarded as one of the greatest military leaders and tacticians in history. Perhaps military historians should occasionally step back and consider whether the slaughter of 17 million mostly unarmed people (about 5% of the world's population) is really worthy of praise in any category. Anyway, Timur conquered most of Western Asia and amongst many other atrocities reputedly had 70,000 human heads built up into minarets, which is an interesting way to honour the religion of peace.

By referring to himself as the Sword of Islam, Timur hinted as to his motivation to conquer the world, and was the last of the great nomadic despots before the Ottoman and Safavid Empires took over the job of decimating the hemisphere in the name of their lord. Whether it was his religion that caused him to commit atrocities or whether he merely used religion as an excuse for his psychopathy will never be known for sure. What is known is that millions of people across Asia are now subjected to the almost never ending wail of the call to prayer to celebrate an Arabian trader who heard voices and who also had a bit of an appetite for brutal conquest.

Religion was once again cited in the commission of mass atrocities in 1553, this time in Britain. Although the reign of Bloody Mary (Queen Mary1) was fairly short, just 5 years, her decision to switch back to Catholicism (so she could marry a royal Philip from Spain), nevertheless resulted in the murder of hundreds of Protestants, most of whom were burnt at the stake.

"Oooh did you hear the news? The Queen's getting married."

"Oooooh, really? Who's the lucky fella?"

"Some bloke from Spain."

"Spain?"

"Yeah, Spai… Oh shit."

"Shit's right. They're all Catholics, aren't they?"

"Yeah. Oh, well. I hope we at least get to see the wedding before she torches us."

Public displays of barbaric cruelty have been so popular down the ages it seems surprising that a reality TV show hasn't reintroduced some form of mass torture as entertainment. Involving the participants that is, rather than merely inflicting shite-as-entertainment on accidental viewers. Although there are some shows, including Japanese ones that make people swim with snakes and eat Chihuahua Spiders and the like, so I guess they're trying.

I read about a planned Russian show that would involve humans hunting each other, but I don't know if it was ever actually produced. They would all sign waivers that allowed for other players to kill them without any legal recourse, sort of like a Hunger Games with food I suppose, though I haven't seen the Hunger Games so I can't be sure about that. Which brings us to Russia.

In 1917, in St Petersburg, the October Revolution overturned the provisional government that had replaced Tsar

Nicholas II. Vladimir Lenin, the instigator of the coup, soon emerged as leader of the Soviet Union. Lenin deemed it necessary to rid the land of political opponents and so he unleashed the Red Terror along with the associated Decossackization progrom, which permanently removed hundreds of thousands of Cossacks along with the testicles of a touring Scottish football team that had the misfortune of being in the prefecture of a short-sighted administrator when the telegram arrived. The fourth division team, Bagforth United, is still holding out for an apology to this day. Another Vladimir unofficially put in his response in 2019 through a spokesperson saying that it would be beneath him and the horse he rode in on to ever apologise for any reason to a group of nutless wonders. Lenin was irresponsible for perhaps half a million murders in his time at the top, a record quickly made to appear sissy-like by his successor.

One of the reasons that there's so much debate over the number of people murdered by Joseph Stalin is that there were too many to count. As in too many millions. Scholars ask whether he should he be credited with those who died of starvation as well as those more deliberately targeted. Yes is the answer to that. Not difficult really. Perhaps if he'd pretended to give a shit it might be worth thinking about.

2.5 million deaths were officially recorded in the Gulags. Given that there's not a lot of upside for serial killers keeping records, that's a number that might be regarded as a very conservative minimum.

The Holodomor (a real thing, and therefore much, much more horrible than Voldemort or Mordor), is also known as the Terror-Famine or the Great Famine, and was the deliberate genocide of the Ukrainian people by means of starvation in 1932. That's not so long ago, so it's not hard to find photographs of Ukrainians lying dead in the street, with others walking past. What could they do? They weren't strong enough to pick them up. They were starving too. Starving to such an extent that they were driven to cannibalism. Eat the dead or die was the choice forced upon millions of people. It was their only choice. 7 to 10 million Ukrainians died of starvation.

Stalin also carried out the great purge of the intelligentsia, the government and the armed forces. Anyone with the ability to pose any threat to Stalin, real or imagined, was sent to the Gulags, never to return. Stalin ruled from 1922 to 1953, and although it was unlikely to have been his initial plan to starve Ukrainians to death, it was his policies and his mismanagement that directly led to the the grain shortages that led to the mass starvation.

Quentin Crisp once said that there was no point in dusting and cleaning because after four years it doesn't get any worse. Perhaps that's how Stalin felt after killing his first few million people. Many millions had to go on suffering under him, watching their friends and neighbours die or disappear, for over 30 years.

It's really no wonder that Russians aren't the people you're most likely to have a few laughs with at the pool bar in Ibiza. Life as they know it is nothing like life as we know it. And never has been. In a jungle, if you're not a predator, you're prey.

It could be argued that Russia has been under despotic rule since… well since pretty much forever. Whoever's been in charge has seen to it that the peasants have always been shat on. Whether it was the Tsars, Lenin, Stalin, or Putin, Russians have suffered under the thumb of brutal rulers. They glimpsed a brief crack of light in 1991 when the Communist Party lost control and they almost turned into a democracy, but within ten years Putin had taken control and that was the end of that.

Adolf Hitler is often cited as the baby most likely to be killed by a time traveller, but as bad he was, and he was seriously bad, he's just one of many nasty, murderous despots who killed as many people as they could. The alarming thing is that despots are like world champion sports people, in that there's only room for so many at the top. And for every champion, there are thousands of like-minded souls working their hardest to get to be the one at the top. The one with the power to point at someone and have them killed. I mean win the race.

Hitler's reign lasted 12 years. His crazy plan to defeat the whole world finally crashed around his ears and in order to avoid humiliation at a level that would have been totally unbearable for a narcissist, he topped himself. He popped a cap in his own ass. Or he had Eva pop a thumb in his ass. Whatever. He didn't emerge from the bunker. His plan to create a master race only got as far as cremating Jews, Slavs, gypsies, homosexuals and political opponents. Despite his ultimate failure, his Nazis managed to kill about 11 million people all up. About a million a year.

Although Hitler's troops wore the slogan "Gott mit uns" on their belt buckles, and he had, along with Mussolini, the tacit approval of the Roman Catholic Church, it would be a huge stretch to blame Hitler's antics on religious fervour. His hatred of Jews was not really balanced by any serious love of Christianity or anything other than himself. It was just hate. He was a common or garden malignant narcissist with side dollops of sadism, sociopathy and psychopathy and probably a few more personality disorders in varying degrees. A nasty little insecure, racist bigot, with delusions of grandeur that sadly became reality for a few years.

Mao Zedong, one of the founders of the Chinese Communist Party, was a scholar of Marx and Lenin although his death stats are closer to those of Stalin. Somewhere between 40 and 80 million people perished under his rule which lasted from 1943 to 1976. Mao's fans, and there were many, credit him with modernising China, although his Great Leap Forward, changing the economy from an agrarian to an industrial one, only really established that food grown in fields is more nourishing than widgets made in smelly factories, as millions of dead people would attest. Like other dictators he also cleared out intellectuals and other "counter-revolutionary elements", meaning that he murdered everybody who could possibly pose a threat to him. As is the way of the despot.

Idi Amin declared himself president after leading a military coup against the elected government of Uganda in 1971. He went on to kill up to half a million of his subjects over the next 8 years, and purportedly ate a few of them, before being ousted to live in luxurious exile in Saudi Arabia for the rest of his life. He had no concerns about being made to answer for his murderous behaviour while living in Jeddah, knowing that the Saudis were big fans of butchery and sadistic brutality. True to type, Amin was a bigot and quite happy to terrorise people purely on the basis of race. His chosen scapegoats were Uganda's Asian residents (mostly Indian and Pakistani citizens), who were driven out or otherwise disposed of if they didn't move quickly enough.

When Britain finally had enough of him in 1977 (patience is not always a virtue) and broke off diplomatic relations, Amin declared victory, and awarded himself the CBE (Conqueror of the British Empire). His full title was, "His Excellency, President for Life, Field Marshal Al Hadji Doctor Idi Amin Dada, VC, DSO, MC, CBE, Lord of All the Beasts of the Earth and Fishes of the Seas and Conqueror of the British Empire in Africa in General and Uganda in Particular". He also claimed to be the uncrowned King of Scotland. Insanity is not a barrier to attaining power, although it should be.

This section is getting too long, and it's a bit depressing, so we'd better move on to the main course, the undisputed champions of despotic terror regime enforcement. Just before we do that, it's worth noting that other contenders such as Augusto Pinochet, Saddam Hussein (arguably the most sadistically evil individual of all time), Pol Pot, Ivan the Terrible, Robespierre, Baby Doc Duvalier, Nicolae Ceausescu, Mussolini, The Kim Jongs, the Saudi hipster known as MBS, Robert Mugabe, Caligula, Enver Pasha, Oliver Cromwell, Leopold II, Vlad the Impaler and many, many more, have the credentials to easily feature here.

But. Easily out-playing, out-thinking, out-torturing, out-killing and out-lasting all opposition is The Holy Roman Catholic Church, the undisputed world champions of long form despotic reigns of terror. Namely, the Inquisition. Most despotic regimes last no longer than the individual asshole who started it. In fact no longer than the few years they can hold out before some other asshole deposes them, usually somewhere between 5 and 40 years. But the gangsters of the

Holy See terrorised Europe for not one hundred, not two hundred, not three hundred but six hundred and fifty years. That's more than twenty generations. That such an abomination could terrorise a continent for so long is really hard to comprehend, but the records are there. It happened. Humanity should be ashamed.

And especially ashamed that the institution that perpetrated the most despicable reign of terror in the history of the world not only still exists, but has exalted tax-free status, and has continued to hoodwink, plunder and rape the children of the poor and gullible, without pause, ever since. We should also be ashamed that most, if not all of the world's largest, richest and most corrupt organisations are based on hypocrisy and lies such as the afterlife, and the ability to control what happens to people who go there.

The Holocaust was an absolute atrocity by any measure. It was as vile and as horrific an event as can possibly be imagined. It lasted for about four years. Those four years were certainly worse for Jews and other targets of the Nazis than any four period of the Inquisition, but thankfully the Holocaust ended. And many of the perpetrators were caught and punished.

The terror for those who lived through the Inquisition was never ending. Literally. It was there as a potential catastrophe that could destroy them and their families, at any moment, for their entire lives. As it had been for their parents, their grandparents and so on. And would be for their children and their grand children and on and on. For twenty generations. Monty Python characters famously said, "Nobody expects the Spanish Inquisition." Except they did. Like the baker who had a disagreement with the farmer who he subsequently saw talking to the priest. Would the farmer bear false witness and call him a heretic? If he did, the baker might get a knock on the door a week or two months later and a few people would be tortured to death as a result. Or the woman who liked cats. God forbid she was seen petting a black one by someone who didn't like her.

It was like living in the moment, if that moment was in primary school in New Zealand when a classmate returned from the dental clinic (1930s-1980s), a small building affectionately known as the murder house, a place where a power cut did not mean no drilling today, it meant the use of the foot-cranked, rubber-band-driven drill. If the nurse's leg got a bit tired and she failed to pedal with enough pressure, the drill would graunch to a halt, possibly getting jammed in a tooth. The terror in the classroom peaked at the moment a child with a swollen jaw appeared at the door and announced that the the dental nurse would like to see… It was a feeling of dread, which for residents of southern Europe lasted your whole life.

The Languedoc is a beautiful region in the south of France. It's where the terror began in 1184. Popes had their minions build them fantastic grand residences and cathedrals in the best positions in beautiful cities and towns including the

Palais des Papes (Palace of the Popes), a massive palace, castle and cathedral complex in Avignon, the name of which was a pretty clear demonstration of how the Catholic crime bosses regarded themselves. From their magnificent headquarters the godfathers spread the enforcement of their rules far and wide.

By the end of the Middle Ages, England and Castile, a region in central Spain, were the only places in Europe without a papal inquisition. Though life wouldn't have been very much better there for most people. Those with the power, from local landlords through to Kings, were mostly despots to some degree because there was nothing stopping them. Not even their so-called religious beliefs. Because that's another thing that despots and demagogues have in common - a large measure of hypocrisy.

It's easy to imagine that a poorly designed human brain might occasionally malfunction in a way that would produce sadism and psychopathy. But history suggests that when there's a reasonable chance of escaping punishment for such behaviour, an alarming number of humans are more than willing to join in. And not just in a wild heat of the moment situation. Much of what occurred, and still occurs today, requires a lot of thinking and planning.

The Turkish bone saw massacre of Jamal Khashoggi required a large amount of planning that involved flying a team of Saudi government assassins on a private jet to Istanbul, a stopover in Egypt to pick up some obviously very special murder potion, with which to inject Khashoggi before subjecting him to strangulation, stabbings and dismemberment. If a nasty despot is prepared to give the murder of one opponent that much malice aforethought, imagine how much time he's happy to devote to the planning of the suffering of multitudes.

Popes devoted a great deal of time to the consideration of the practice of torture. Pope Innocent IV's papal bull of 1252, explicitly authorised and defined the appropriate circumstances for the use of torture in extracting confessions from heretics. One prominent inquisitor almost threw a spaniard in the works by declaring that confessions obtained by torture are misleading and futile. (Whilst widely accepted by experts, this opinion regarding the effectiveness of torture has been mostly ignored. Possibly because, like war, so many men get off on it.) There was some concern amongst inquisitors that over zealous use of torture outside of papal guidelines may be punishable by torture, but that problem was overcome in 1256 when the boss of bosses decreed that inquisitors would be given absolution if they used instruments of torture.

And so it was that those so inclined, possibly ancestors of Douglas McDonnell, Ray Theon, Graeme Northrop and Martin Lockheed, set about the design and manufacture of maiming and killing machines. The more horrendous the better. That there were so many different medieval torture devices should be another source of human shame.

Mariotino Dinoguini was regarded as the Heath Robinson of his time, although not of course at the time as he died in 1412. He was posthumously awarded the Michelangelo Inventors Award in the over complex geometric contraption division, at a ceremony held in St Peter's Square in 1972. Although many of the more common forms of torture are of unknown origin, it is likely that Dinoguini had a hand some of the more hideous ones.

Strappado involves the victim's hands being tied behind his back before he's hoist off the ground by his arms. If his shoulder sockets did not dislocate, the torturers might lift and drop him or add weights until they did. A more sadistic version of dislocation torture was the rack, or the Rackardo, as Dinoguini called his versions of it. Dinoguini may not have invented the original rack but he was responsible for the addition of gearing mechanisms on the rollers at each end so that an inquisitor could apply increasing pressure gradually, thus drawing out the duration of the ever increasing pain without the inquisitor having to exert himself or risk breaking a sweat. When using the Dinoguini Rackardo XL, a priest could apply sufficient pressure to tear off the arms (or legs whichever came first) of the accused heretic with but a single finger on the handle, such was the excellence of the engineering.

For instances of insufficient screaming, Dinoguini recommended the application of additional pain centres by means of thumbscrews, foot clamps, metal pincers, pliers, and red hot pokers, a favourite of many priests especially when plunged into the anal cavity of the suspect, which is where the interests of the priests invariably ended up.

Mutilation was technically forbidden, though Pope Alexander IV, in his decree of 1256, declared that inquisitors could absolve each other of any wrongdoing that may have occurred during torture sessions.

Tomas de Torquemada, the first Grand Inquisitor of the Spanish Inquisition, was particularly fond of the rack and especially Dinoguini's Rackardo XL, often regaling other sadists with its performance benefits over other stretching devices such as the horse (sort of like a pommel horse, but with ropes) and the wheel (sort of like a water wheel but with ropes). A little known fact is that it was Torquemada's vivid descriptions of the amount of turning force required to dislodge a limb, that led to the use of the term "torque" as a measure of twisting power that's still used to this day as a measure of engine performance.

One fiendishly nasty torture machine that was not invented by Dinoguini was the Brazen Bull. It was a life-size brass statue of a bull, hollow with a trapdoor and enough space inside for a man. A victim was placed inside the bull and then a fire was set below the belly of the beast. Often the victim had his tongue cut out so as to make the human nature of the screams less obvious, as the intention was for the bull to seem to be alive as the burning man writhed around inside, initially trying to avoid touching the hottest parts, and then thrashing about in agony. As the victim was cooked alive, smoke was emitted through the beast's nostrils.

The Brazen Bull was invented by a Greek called Perilaus, who expected to be well paid well when he presented his masterpiece to his local despot, Phalaris of Agrigentum. It would be many centuries before it would be possible for a malignant narcissist to throw his sycophants under a bus, so Phalaris, clearly a real piece of work, instead threw Perilaus into the Brazen Bull for its first official test run. As often happened with despots, Phalaris was eventually overthrown and was reputedly disposed of inside the same Brazen Bull.

Another invention re-engineered by Mariotino Dinoguini was the Iron Maiden, a sort of upright coffin with spikes inside that impaled the soon-to-be corpse placed inside it. Dinoguini thought it would a bit of a laugh to make the maiden look like the Virgin Mary, and have spikes on the insides of her arms so that when a wheel was turned to cause Mary's arms to embrace the enclosed victim, the spikes would gradually impale them. An English heavy metal band formerly known as The Brazen Hussies was re-named Iron Maiden after the drummer's mother, despairing of having to suffer through their practice sessions, declared that she'd rather spend the next hour in an Iron Maiden rather than another hour listening to them.

The Scavenger's Daughter was a large iron hoop that was placed around a body in the fetal position, and once again used increasing compression as a means of titillating sadists. The Breast Ripper was a device used on the fairer sex. Basically a metal claw utilised as its name suggests. Women haven't been mentioned much in this section but they were often treated in even more barbaric ways than men.

Although many believed that Dinoguini was a common or garden sadist there is some evidence that he actually thought that he was doing the right thing, that he was acting in the service of a higher power. Whilst perusing the 1578 edition of the Directorium Inquisitorum (the standard manual of the Inquisition) he was disturbed to read the passage about the official purpose of inquisitorial penalties. "Punishment does not take place primarily and per se for the correction and good of the person punished, but for the public good in order that others may become terrified and weaned away from the evils they would commit." Dinoguini decided to discuss it with his local Inquisitor. Why he thought that was a good idea is anybody's guess, and the meeting certainly didn't go as he must have imagined it might.

Dinoguini: The manual says that the point of the torture in interrogation is that others may become terrified.

Inquisitor: Yeah, and?

Dinoguini: The point is to terrorise people?

Inquisitor: Yep. It's in the manual. Official policy.

Dinoguini: I thought the purpose was to expose heretics, not to terrorise.

Inquisitor: You naive little ponce. Of course it's to make people terrified. Who the fuck do you think you're dealing with? Have you never heard the term God-fearing Christian?

Dinoguini: Well, yeah.

Inquisitor: And the threat of the fires of hell for all eternity?

Dinoguini: Yeah.

Inquisitor: And the idea that God is watching over you and can read your every thought, and he knows when you touch yourself in the sexy way?

Dinoguini: Uh huh.

Inquisitor: What might be the point of all that do you think?

Dinoguini: To make people afraid?

Inquisitor: Exactly. To keep people in a constant state of fear. So that they will pay their tithe every week and obey the will of the church at all times.

Dinoguini: Yeah but I don't think I want to be part of a terrorist organisation.

Inquisitor: Hey, what the fuck? Who the fuck are you calling a terrorist organisation, you miserable little shit?

Dinoguini: Ah… didn't you just say…

Inquisitor: Are you calling the Holy Roman Catholic

Church a terrorist organisation?

Dinoguini: Ah... no... I... no...

Inquisitor: Sounds like heresy to me.

Dinoguini: Wait I... I didn't mean...

Inquisitor: You, my son, have just booked yourself a ticket to the torture chamber.

Dinoguini: Oh, fuck me.

Inquisitor: Oh we will do that, my son, we will do that. You will be soundly dealt with.

Dinoguini: Jesus Christ.

Inquisitor: He won't help you now you snivelling little piece of rat shit. All you'll be getting is the embrace of the spiky loving arms of the Virgin Mary.

And so it came to pass that the Inquisitor called in his buddies and together they devised an inquisition tailor-made for Dinoguini. They decided to subject him to a sample treatment from each one of the devices he had a hand in either designing or modifying, and then to ask him which one he'd least like to have another taste of.

Despite the dire situation he was in Dinoguini gave some thought as to how he should rate the pain of each device. He told the inquisition members that he would to try to rate the pain level of each device on a scale of one to ten, with one being barely troublesome and ten being unbearable agony. This is the same system used to this day in hospitals and medical practices all around the world. It was formerly known as the Dinoguini Pain Scale, but his name was dropped after nurses tired of having to explain its origin.

In the first round of his torture Dinoguini tragically let himself down, the inquisition team down, and his home town down, by screaming ten ten ten on every device, despite only moderate amounts of pressure being applied. He apologised but said in his defence that he could not have imagined that every single one of the torture devices would produced more pain than he thought was ever possible.

Accordingly the inquisitors decided to give him a second full round on the machines, this time with the dials turned up a notch. Between screams, Dinoguini managed to cry out numbers between twelve and seventeen. One of the witnesses, who were officially there as observers of record, but who had in fact paid big bucks to watch, was mathematician Stefano Hawkintino, who said, by way of conversation, that it was ridiculous to give scores of 12 or 17 out of ten. It just didn't make sense. It was like those stupid oafs at the sporting spectacles in the Colosseum saying they were giving 110%.

The mathematician was immediately accused of suggesting heretical mathematical scientific ideas in defiance of established Vatican standards. He was strapped to a torture device and given repeated opportunities to rethink and repent his position, but the pain apparently overwhelmed his ability to reason clearly enough to remember his safe word and he remained alongside Dinoguini for the final moments of his penance to his sweet loving lord and master.

It seems fitting, having examined various aspects of the human brain as a creation of God, ranging from the best to the worst traits, we arrived at the despotism of malignant narcissists as being the undisputed champion of the worst of the worst of all possible human behaviours, and further that the absolute champions of despotism are also God's champions.

Which almost seems to support the idea that God, the God of the Old Testament, the almighty, malignant, narcissistic despot himself, designed the human brain in his own image. But that would require the Old Testament to be plausible. So, nah.

The Narcissist Problem

Whilst researching the stuff about despots, it became apparent that a huge proportion of the world's problems are caused by a small number of people with recognisable personality disorders. Malignant narcissists with sociopathic tendencies.

If humanity is going to advance, the most important thing we can do is to figure out a way to identify these people and disqualify them from attaining positions of power in public life. It might a good job for a Benevolent Artificial General Intelligence.

It sounds almost horrendous to invoke psychological profiling, like a Clockwork Orange or thought police or Nazi Eugenics but the aim would not be to eliminate people from society, or even to sterilise them, although... No. The aim would be to prevent them from holding senior levels of authority which may have the potential to be injurious to society in malignant hands.

If malignant narcissists could be permanently banished from power, the world would have a very good chance of developing into a decent place for everybody to live. Provided there was also, as imagined by John Lennon, no religion.

Summary of the Human Brain

So there it is. The human brain.

An organ whose greatest strength is also its greatest weakness.

Our greatest strength, the thing that separates us from all other animals is the ability to make stuff up, to create abstract ideas and to communicate those ideas to others along with being able to understand incoming ideas. Our greatest weakness is our limited ability to reliably discern whether that incoming information is true or false.

As children we accept the fantasy fictions told to us by our parents and then we accept that they were just a story when we get a bit older.

Young Boy : Yeah, mom, I see that whole Santa Claus thing was really implausible. Like how could he possibly go to every house in the world in one night? And why didn't he bring any presents to all those starving kids in Africa? Not even a Christmas dinner. And yeah that tooth fairy thing. What would she do all the rest of the time? Just fly around waiting for kids' teeth to fall out? Just so obviously crazy. I don't know why we ever believed that. And that one about an old man with a beard up in the clouds coming down and having a baby with a virgin and then drowning everybody on earth and millions of animals from all over the world all getting on one boat and not eating each other. Woo hoo. What a whopper. Who knows why we fell for that one.

Mother : Hold on son. That last one's still true.

Young Boy : What? Nah. Get outta here.

On one hand the human brain is a computer of amazing complexity and awesome power.

On the other hand, it's a neurotic stumbling mess that has a huge amount of trouble distinguishing shit from Shinola. Some human brains are just plain stupid. Others are really smart by certain measures but they still believe crazy things like conspiracy theories, ridiculous cults and the free hand of trickle-down economics.

It's hard to believe the human brain was created by a perfect God as the perfect thinking machine to control his perfectly created creature. As well as its brilliance it has so many flaws one could be excused for thinking it might have developed the way it has from some sort of random natural process. Such as evolution.

If God created the human brain, then surely the human brain would have been programmed to follow only him, the one true God, rather than having a strong tendency to follow all manner of random crazy cults. After all, isn't that what the God of the Bible demands in his first commandment? Why command that level of obedience from your own created creatures, then program the brains of your flock to be equally likely to prefer some other one of thousands of false gods? Or none at all?

Because mysterious ways? Because free will? Why demand obedience then assign free will? It's like an Army General commanding his cavalry to charge at the enemy but when they ride off in all directions he just shrugs his shoulders.

Given all that it seems quite likely that God was in fact created by the human brain.

So let's have a look at the God of the Bible, and think about the type of God that man, pre-industrial man, would imagine such a God to be.

Part Two

starring

God

as the

creation of

The Human Brain

God

Which God? There've been so many.

This part of the book was going to be introduced with a list of Gods, but that's not so easy to do. There are far too many to name. Even counting them isn't straight forward. When you ask Google how many Gods there are, or have been, the results are anything but definitive. Throughout history every culture, every tribe, every locale, every local, every football team, has had its own Gods. There have been anywhere from many thousands to a few million Gods and almost the same number of religions to go with them. The absolute minimum sensible answer to the number of gods seems to be a few thousand.

A few thousand Gods. In earlier times most people were polytheists, worshiping multiple gods, but as a result of the conquests of the armed forces of the Abrahamic religions, monotheists are more common today. Monotheists believe that all of these thousands of gods are the creation of the human mind except for the one they believe in, which is real. Atheists agree with that but without that single exception, not even for the god their parents told them was the real one.

It's interesting to think that believers, people of faith, know that all those thousands of gods that they don't believe in were created by human minds. That they were imagined into existence, like James Bond or Harry Potter. Believers know

247

that. What else could they think? It's the only explanation for a god that's not real. Someone made it up. Yet despite the striking similarity of the one they believe is real to the many they know for certain are fictional, they still think their one is real. How faith survives the overwhelming obviousness of the fictional nature of gods is a mystery to those of us looking in from outside the cult, whichever one it may be.

Small diversion - I use the word cult deliberately because the only real difference between a cult and a religion is the number of followers. Imagine if the Catholic Church had never existed. Now imagine a group of a hundred or so people who gather at some kind of movie ranch in California with a small church building in which they hold services where the priest is dressed in long, flamboyant robes and wears a tall golden hat, and boys, dressed in flowing white dresses, swing smoking metal spheres from chains and then everyone is given a morsel representing the flesh of a sort of dead but not dead god, who's part of a triple god, and a sip of wine that magically turns into the actual blood of that sort of not really dead part of the triple god. Would you call that a church or a cult? Probably a death cult given the statue of the bleeding god-zombie on a cross that they bow down before.

The fact that there are at least a few thousand Gods is pretty close to enough information to conclude that all Gods are indeed the creation of mankind. What's more likely? There a few thousand imaginary Gods for whom there is no verifiable evidence, or there are a few thousand imaginary Gods and one real God, who is indistinguishable from all the imaginary ones (except for his believers) and for whom there is also no verifiable evidence?

What's more likely? There's a herd of a few thousand wildebeest none of whom can speak English, or there's a herd of a few thousand wildebeest one of whom can speak English, but the evidence for that is only hearsay? And that English speaking wildebeest lived a thousand years ago. On the moon.

There are times when it's a natural human reaction to pray, even for non-believers. Such as when there's an earthquake, or the wind's about to tear the roof off, when the plane's about to crash, or when you discover that there's a whole lot more misery to seasickness than mere nausea. The prayer of the non-believer is something like "Please, please, make it better. Please, please, please. Make it stop." The prayer is to no God in particular, or in fact to no God at all. It's more of a natural terror reflex than a prayer. But it does suggest why so much prayer is fear-based. A good Christian is a God-fearing Christian.

It's no surprise that severe wind, rain, thunder and lightning resulted in Gods of scary things being invented. In fact they were probably prayed to before they were invented, and that's how they were invented. Gods of almost anything else you can think of were also invented although many of the old single issue Gods have gone out of fashion, at least in the west. If you say that those Gods were obviously creations of the human brain now that they've lost their believers, you'll get no argument from anyone. So there'd be no point in dwelling on them.

So which God should we mostly consider here?

Most of the potential readers of this book will be familiar with the God of Abraham, as depicted in the Bible, and billions of people believe in some version of that god so it makes sense to concentrate mostly on him.

(Also I know very little about any of the other gods, but I'd be mightily surprised if the general point made here, that it's all fictional bullshit, did not apply to all of them equally.)

God - In His Own Write

(That's a nod to John Lennon)

The Bible starts at "the beginning" - in which God, through the pens and quills of his human transcribers, tries to explain who and what he is.

"In the beginning God created the heavens and the earth."

Those are the first words of the old testament. Nothing precedes them. There's no attempt to explain what God was doing for possibly billions and billions of years that preceded "the beginning" and it's easy to understand why. Because like pretty much everything that follows in these ancient writings, it doesn't make any sense at all.

In the beginning God created... For that to have any chance of making sense, it means that God pre-existed the beginning. God pre-existed existence. How long had God existed before he began creating? A millisecond? A million years? God's book doesn't say. It just says that God was already there at the beginning. Already there. Where he came from, how long he'd been there and why he came is a mystery. And not the only one. When there's nothing there and nothing's happening, is there any difference between a millisecond and a million years? God only knows. But he chose not to include that information in his book.

The faithful have been heard to say that God exists outside of space and time. Whatever the fuck that might mean. Try explaining that as if to a child. The fact that it's impossible to explain in any way that makes sense to a normal, intelligent human mind might be the clue that leads to the deduction that it doesn't make sense. To anybody. It's a cop out. Like mysterious ways.

Something not existing in space is understandable. The Twin Towers of the World Trade Centre no longer exist in space but they used to and they still occupy a place in time. Something that doesn't exist in time is another matter. If it doesn't exist in time, that means it doesn't exist now, it never existed before now, and it never will exist in the future, which is another way of saying it doesn't exist. Never has, never will. Apart from possibly in someone's imagination. Which is, coincidentally, the best description of everything about God.

Outside of time means not here with us in the time that humanity exists, and in all the time prior to our existence, and off out into the future. It means never. Never was, never will be. Never.

Outside of space means not here in the space where we exist. Not in any part of it. Not in any part of it right out beyond the edges of the Milky Way. Nowhere. Nowhere at all.

In order to interact with humans on earth a thing from outside of space and time would have to cross over, perhaps through a wormhole. And then leave again. To go where? Nowhere? No place? With no physical presence?

Something that doesn't exist physically, doesn't exist here, never has, and never will, can only be imaginary. A special kind of imaginary that's actually real, but can't be explained or even understood. Which could almost serve as a definition of woo woo. That which sounds profound but actually means nothing. All icing, no cake. Except for the icing. Which is also imaginary. No icing, no cake. No thing. Nothing. Never.

If it were somehow possible for God to exist outside of time and space, then what's up with the Bible? It's full of tales of God in our time and space. Shouldn't it be, "God exists outside of time and space except for the time written about in his big book where he invaded our space and time to impregnate the virgin and all that stuff. And then he left our time and space, never to return."

If you believe any of that might in any way be true, it would seem like the story ends when God abandons us by stepping back out of our time and space. Many Christians talk about the second coming, but when they look hopefully to the heavens for signs of the rapture they're a billion times more likely to see a squirt of pigeon shit about to hit them in the face.

If the Bible was a brand new story being pitched to a studio exec in Hollywood, the end of that famous first sentence is the point at which the exec might raise a hand, palm towards the hopeful pitcher and say, hold up a second, what's the backstory of this God character? And when the answer is that he's always just been there, like forever, doing absolutely nothing for an infinite amount of time, or perhaps, he's a mysterious character who exists in mysterious ways outside of time and space, those pitching the story might be told to go away and do a bit more work on it. (Though probably not. There are plenty of movies with gaping plot holes. Many humans don't object to a lack of logic.)

A commonly held position amongst those of faith is that nothing can exist without being created, and therefore everything needs a creator. Except apparently for the creator who didn't need a creator to be created because… the creator works in mysterious ways. And the answer is God. Pretty much regardless of the question.

Whether Satan or the Devil were supposed to have existed at this stage or whether he/they needed to be created by the creator is unclear. (To me at least.) I think there's a passage in the Bible that says God created the devil, but there'll probably be another passage that contradicts it so I'll leave that to theologians. Imagine spending your whole life analysing Harry Potter books or the Lord of the Rings, but looking for hidden meanings whilst believing it's all true. That's theology. At least you're allowed to say you don't care for fantasy fiction without being accused of not knowing enough about it to have a valid opinion. Or to be killed for that opinion.

What is clear is that we are expected to believe that God pulled off the most incredible magic trick of all time and created himself, the one and only god, the omniscient, the omnipotent, the omnipresent one, out of nothing. If God was preceded by anything else then he's not the creator of everything.

Some Christians attempt to mock atheists by claiming that atheists believe that the universe was created spontaneously out of nothing. Which is top level projection. Atheism makes no claims. All atheism does is call bullshit. It says I don't believe your wacky stories. Christians claim, in the first sentence of their book, that in the beginning God created everything. Including himself perhaps. Out of what? Nothing. Presumably. It was the beginning. There was nothing there. Big claim. No evidence. Bullshit.

I find it incomprehensible that the universe was created out of nothing, or almost nothing, or compacted something, or whatever, by the big bang. Or anything else. But at least I'm not threatened with eternal torture and damnation if I admit to being unconvinced on account of being unable to get my human brain around the concept.

That the universe is here now is indisputable. (Except of course to those bamboozled and befuddled by peddlers of quantum soup semantics. But let's not waste time on bullshit of the woo woo ilk.) Where the universe came from is a mystery. That it might have always been there is as hard to comprehend as what might have been happening half an hour before the big bang. But that mystery cannot be explained by someone simply making shit up. Especially a story as risible as the nonsense in the Bible.

"I don't understand it, therefore God", seems to satisfy many millions of people, but it's a vile abuse of the word therefore.

What's more likely? From nothing came this random exploding mass of matter that formed galaxies and solar systems, or from nothing came an all seeing, all-knowing, all creating, all powerful God? At least we know the matter part is real because we can see it, feel it, breath it, eat it and excrete it. We are it. The second option, alas, is undetectable by any means other than the human imagination.

Neither of these scenarios are truly understandable or comprehensible by a normal human brain. Like the concept of the size of the universe. Think about it too long and your brain will hurt and eventually explode.

The big bang premise requires, like quantum mechanics, that we accept it because it seems to explain things to physicists, even though nobody understands it well enough to be able to clearly explain it "as if to a child", as the saying goes. But apart from that small leap of faith, everything we observe about the universe around us makes sense in a way consistent with scientific theory. Perhaps not quite everything. Yet. There's still plenty left to discover and learn.

To accept the second premise requires that we believe in some mythical power that works in mysterious ways for which there is absolutely no evidence except for some fantastical stories written a long time ago. Stories which contain a lot of information that we now know to be absolutely, fundamentally wrong. The only place in the universe where things involving powerful, magical, spiritual forces can be found are in the faith of religious believers, in the works of fantasy writers, in movies and on TV, and in the brains of children.

A God who works in mysterious ways is another way of saying "I don't know the reason God does that" or more simply, "I don't know." Why have a belief system that whenever a difficult question gets asked the answer is "it's a mystery" or "I don't know" when you could approach the whole God question with "I don't know".

What we do know is that the scientific explanations are a whole lot more plausible than the stories in the bible. Wait, that's not quite right. The scientific explanations are not only plausible, they are verifiable. That's what makes then scientific. And true. The stories in the Bible are neither plausible nor verifiable.

Let's take another look at the "everything needs a creator" schtick. The only realistic suspect as the creator of God is the human mind. God certainly exists in the brains of humanity. Does he exist anywhere else? There's no plausible evidence for that. Only faith and belief. Nothing tangible. If the human brain is the only place where God definitely exists, does that mean he was also created there? Stands to reason. There's no evidence that he wasn't.

And what about the alternative, that God created himself out of nothing. The universe has a massive amount of empty space where gods could spontaneously create themselves at any moment. But it never happens. Apart from that one time. By the God your parents were told to believe in by their parents.

Enough of that. We won't spend so long on the second sentence. Or even the second half of the first sentence.

The Book Of Genesis

When regarding the God of the Bible, it makes sense to start at the beginning, which means Genesis, the first book of the Old Testament, which forms the basis of Christianity, Islam and Judaism. God does a fair bit of talking to himself in this part and gives himself grades of "good" and "very good" for his work.

With regard to the likelihood of God being actually God, rather than a creation of man, it's instructive to consider God's understanding of the physical reality of the universe he supposedly created. The official story of how God created the universe makes it abundantly clear that whoever inspired or wrote the blessed words had no more understanding of the nature of the universe and our solar system than your average household cat.

The italicised passages below are direct quotes from the Old Testament, although the number and variety of different translations and versions of the Bible makes the concept of a direct quote somewhat questionable. Anyway, let's get into it.

Genesis 1   The Beginning

In the beginning God created the heavens and the earth. Now the earth was formless and empty, darkness was over the surface of the deep, and the Spirit of God was hovering over the waters.

And God said, "Let there be light," and there was light. God saw that the light was good, and he separated the light from the darkness. God called the light "day," and the darkness he called "night." And there was evening, and there was morning—the first day.

Creating the entire universe and separating day and night was a very good day's work, but God did not judge himself on the first day.

Also note that creating the heavens and the earth did not include the stars, the sun and the moon. They would come later, more like decoration. Sky ornaments perhaps.

And God said, "Let there be a vault between the waters to separate water from water." So God made the vault and separated the water under the vault from the water above it. And it was so. God called the vault "sky." And there was evening, and there was morning—the second day.

God must have been tired after day one, because all he managed on day two was to separate water from water. Creating the heavens and the earth in a day was gonna be a hard act to follow but really? Hard to say how day and night, or even the earth and the heavens would have looked after the first day with the water and the water still combined as one, but let's not get picky.

Also both God and the person transcribing what God said (who was he talking to and in what language and where did they come from and why did they wait hundreds of years before writing about it anywhere?) seem to believe that the rest of the universe beyond the sky vault is water. Not the sort of error likely to be made by someone who created it.

And God said, "Let the water under the sky be gathered to one place, and let dry ground appear." And it was so. God called the dry ground "land," and the gathered waters he called "seas." And God saw that it was good. Then God said, "Let the land produce vegetation: seed-bearing plants and trees on the land that bear fruit with seed in it, according to their various kinds." And it was so. The land produced vegetation: plants bearing seed according to their kinds and trees bearing fruit with seed in it according to their kinds. And God saw that it was good. And there was evening, and there was morning—the third day.

Another big day. God created land. Rated it as "good". Created plants.

Self-appraisal rating for Day 3 - "good".

He talks to himself a lot… "You talkin' to me? Then who the hell else are you talkin' to? You talkin' to me? Well, I'm the only one here"… which indicates that he'd spent a fair bit of time alone, possibly billions of years, practising in the mirror, rather than creating himself immediately before creating the universe.

And God said, "Let there be lights in the vault of the sky to separate the day from the night, and let them serve as signs to mark sacred times, and days and years, and let them be lights in the vault of the sky to give light on the earth." And it was so. God made two great lights—the greater light to govern the day and the lesser light to govern the night. He also made the stars. God set them in the vault of the sky to give light on the earth, to govern the day and the night, and to separate light from darkness. And God saw that it was good. And there was evening, and there was morning—the fourth day.

God created the stars and the sun and the moon. Another big day. Also separated the light from darkness again, having apparently forgotten that he already did that on day one. Quite how he managed to create the light and separate it from the darkness the first time, three days before creating the sun, remains a mystery.

Self-appraisal rating for Day 4 - "good".

And God said, "Let the water teem with living creatures, and let birds fly above the earth across the vault of the sky." So God created the great creatures of the sea and every living thing with which the water teems and that moves about in it, according to their kinds, and every winged bird according to its kind. And God saw that it was good. God blessed them and said, "Be fruitful and increase in number and fill the water in the seas, and let the birds increase on the earth." And there was evening, and there was morning—the fifth day.

God created all the fish and all the birds and spoke to them, commanding them to go forth and fornicate. They apparently understood him well enough as there's no shortage of fornication in the animal kingdom (except for pandas, who don't seem to fancy other pandas very much, perhaps they should try mating with sloths or capybaras), but the lack of any direct response might have been what gave God the idea to create a species who could talk back to him.

Self-appraisal rating for Day 5 - "good".

And God said, "Let the land produce living creatures according to their kinds: the livestock, the creatures that move along the ground, and the wild animals, each according to its kind." And it was so. God made the wild animals according to their kinds, the livestock according to their kinds, and all the creatures that move along the ground according to their kinds. And God saw that it was good.

Then God said, "Let us make mankind in our image, in our likeness, so that they may rule over the fish in the sea and the birds in the sky, over the livestock and all the wild animals, and over all the creatures that move along the ground."

"Each according to its kind." What the hell does that mean?

Is it the opposite of each individual creature being unique? Mankind has survived as a term, yet fishkind, birdkind and snakekind didn't seem to catch on. "Let us make mankind in our image…" Who is us? And who the hell does he keep talking to? Jesus was not yet a glimmer in his eye. Was his sidekick, the Holy Ghost, created by this time?

So God created mankind in his own image, in the image of God he created them male and female he created them.

God blessed them and said to them, "Be fruitful and increase in number; fill the earth and subdue it. Rule over the fish in the sea and the birds in the sky and over every living creature that moves on the ground."

Then God said, "I give you every seed-bearing plant on the face of the whole earth and every tree that has fruit with seed in it. They will be yours for food. And to all the beasts of the earth and all the birds in the sky and all the creatures that move along the ground—everything that has the breath of life in it—I give every green plant for food." And it was so.

God saw all that he had made, and it was very good. And there was evening, and there was morning—the sixth day.

Created all the animals. Saw that it was good. Created mankind in his own image. Interestingly, the way he allocates the food supplies seems to indicate that he did not realise that he was creating any carnivores or omnivores.

Also, despite having created the entire universe on day 1, and then creating the sun, moon and stars on day 4, he pays no attention to any part of the universe except for planet earth for the rest of the week, or, as far as we know, ever again.

Self-appraisal rating for Day 6 - "very good".

Genesis 2

Thus the heavens and the earth were completed in all their vast array.

By the seventh day God had finished the work he had been doing; so on the seventh day he rested from all his work.

Then God blessed the seventh day and made it holy, because on it he rested from all the work of creating that he had done.

Self-appraisal rating for Day 7 - "takin' it easy".

God put his feet up and had a cold beer. Then he had a few more beers and gave himself a medal. Best God of all time. Of no time. Best God outside of time and space. Supreme God of Neverland.

He was so pleased with himself that he declared every seventh day would forever be held sacred in his honour. Narcissistic much? Pride was apparently not yet a sin.

Could this story possibly get any more ridiculous? Hold my beer, said God. Have you heard the story of Adam and Eve? (Apologies for quoting big chunks of the Bible, but it's sort of necessary to illustrate the point.)

Adam and Eve

This is the account of the heavens and the earth when they were created, when the Lord God made the earth and the heavens.

Now no shrub had yet appeared on the earth and no plant had yet sprung up ...

Hang on a second, what about - *"The land produced vegetation: plants bearing seed according to their kinds and trees bearing fruit with seed in it according to their kinds. And God saw that it was good. And there was evening, and there was morning—the third day."* - Did that happen or not? Did God see trees bearing fruit on day 3? He did a few verses back. Now, not so much. WTF? Are we in a flashback here?

... for the Lord God had not sent rain on the earth and there was no one to work the ground, but streams came up from the earth and watered the whole surface of the ground. Then the Lord God formed a man from the dust of the ground and breathed into his nostrils the breath of life, and the man became a living being.

Hate to be picky but if God wanted to take some dust from the ground shouldn't he have done that before the watering turned it into mud? Anyway...

Now the Lord God had planted a garden in the east, in Eden; and there he put the man he had formed. The Lord God made all kinds of trees grow out of the ground—trees that were pleasing to the eye and good for food. In the middle of the garden were the tree of life and the tree of the knowledge of good and evil.

Okay so those last two trees must have a few readers saying what the fuck? All the other stuff created so far was sort of like real world, but suddenly we're back in a metaverse fantasy land. You just created life, what's the tree of life for? And the good and evil tree is for what? Some kind of squid game?

A river watering the garden flowed from Eden; from there it was separated into four headwaters. The name of the first is the Pishon; it winds through the entire land of Havilah, where there is gold. (The gold of that land is good; aromatic resin and onyx are also there.) The name of the second river is the Gihon; it winds through the entire land of Cush. The name of the third river is the Tigris; it runs along the east side of Ashur. And the fourth river is the Euphrates.

Here the writers realise they've been piling on the bullshit to such an extent they need to take remedial action. A few quasi-realistic sounding geographical details always help when trying to cover over nonsense.

The Lord God took the man and put him in the Garden of Eden to work it and take care of it. And the Lord God commanded the man, "You are free to eat from any tree in the garden; but you must not eat from the tree of the knowledge of good and evil, for when you eat from it you will certainly die."

So there's a tree of life, which doesn't get another mention (maybe it does later on, but this is so silly I probably won't get that far), but the tree of knowledge of good and evil will kill you if you eat from it. Why wasn't it called the tree of death if that's what it does? The man is not going to care about the knowledge of good and evil if he's dead. This is all taking place before any mention of the invention of the afterlife and heaven and hell, so that doesn't come into it here. And why did God put the booby trap in the garden? The only purpose is to cause problems for the man he just created. What a dick move. What a complete asshole.

It's like a sadistic child putting razor blades in a hamster cage.

The Lord God said, "It is not good for the man to be alone. I will make a helper suitable for him."

Here it is. This is where the misogyny kicks in. The misogyny that pervades all the Abrahamic religions. The source of the sometimes brutal subjugation of women in the name of religion for centuries to come. The misogyny that serves as a handbrake on civilisation and personal freedom to this day.

Now the Lord God had formed out of the ground all the wild animals and all the birds in the sky. He brought them to the man to see what he would name them; and whatever the man called each living creature, that was its name. So the man gave names to all the livestock, the birds in the sky and all the wild animals.

But for Adam no suitable helper was found.

Did someone just name Adam? Did Adam name himself like he named all the other animals? Did God think that Adam might find a suitable helper/mate among the other living creatures?

So the Lord God caused the man to fall into a deep sleep; (oh, now he's back to being the man...) *and while he was sleeping, he took one of the man's ribs and then closed up the place with flesh.* (God the surgeon in action. Nurse, pass me a pound of flesh.) *Then the Lord God made a woman from the rib he had taken out of the man, and he brought her to the man.*

If he needed a rib to make a woman, why didn't he need one to make Adam? Or any of the other creatures and potential helpers all of whom were "formed out of the ground"? Mysterious. Moving on.

The man said,

"This is now bone of my bones

and flesh of my flesh;

she shall be called 'woman,'

for she was taken out of man."

That is why a man leaves his father and mother and is united to his wife, and they become one flesh.

Adam and his wife were both naked, and they felt no shame.

Hang on a second. *"That is why a man leaves his father..."* That is why? That explains it in what way? This is Bible logic apparently.

Anyway, although Adam once again is referred to by name, his wife is not yet worthy. Either that or it's just sloppy, or non-existent proofreading and editing.

... and they felt no shame.

Not yet. No prizes for guessing that the bastard who put the booby trap in the Garden of Eden would soon sort that out.

Genesis continued

I very rarely walk out of a movie. Bad movies are sometimes interesting to watch for the mental exercise of analysing the reasons they don't work. But some are too painfully awful even for that. If the Bible were a movie, I'd be halfway home well before the end of Genesis.

The rest of the book of Genesis will be paraphrased rather than quoted for the most part. (Where it is quoted, it is merely to illustrate the crushing tediousness of it so there's no need to read it all, a cursory scan should be enough to get the point.) And then we'll move on to other things.

After creating the universe and everything in it in six days, God declared it was good and rested on the seventh, declaring it to be a day of rest for all time. His ultimate creation, human beings, were told to also regard it as a day of rest, except that it became clear that humans were expected to attend a place of worship where they would kneel before him and praise him and thank him. This ritual of subjugation before the great one every week for your whole life was optional except for the promise of hellfire and eternal damnation if you didn't comply. No rest for the wicked. Or anybody else.

The anthropomorphic nature of God is evident right from the beginning. In this section the moments when God exhibits human traits will be emphasised with **bold characters**.

When he was lonely, God started **talking to himself**. Many of his characteristics are very much like those of humans, often the worst of humans. In declaring that he expected to be praised at least on a weekly basis, he exhibited **extreme narcissism** even bettering that of Turkmenbashy, aka His Excellency Saparmurat Türkmenbaşy, President of Turkmenistan.

Possibly history's second best example of an uncontrollable, raging narcissist was Saparmurat Niyazov, who named himself President For Life and granted himself the title Türkmenbaşhy, meaning Leader Of The Turkmen.

After Turkmenistan gained its independence following the fall of the USSR in 1991, Türkmenbaşhy renamed the second largest city in Turkmenistan, Krasnovodsk, to Türkmenbaşhy in honour of himself. Huge gold statues of Turkmenbashy were erected in nearly every city in Turkmenistan.

Turkmenbashy and God both enjoyed making up rules for those they lorded over, God with his ten commandments and Turkmenbashy with his multitude of decrees which included bans on gold teeth, spandex and opera. As is often the case for a lunatic with absolutely no form of control, self or otherwise, things just kept getting crazier.

In 1997 when he tried to quit smoking he banned smoking in public, to avoid temptation from seeing people smoking on the street. He also ordered all government employees to quit smoking. He had an ice-skating rink built near Ashgabat so the people living in the desert could learn to ice skate. The driving license test required all applicants to pass a morality test.

In 2001 Turkmenbashy published the Ruhnama (The Book of the Soul), which contained stories and poems offering spiritual and moral guidance. He ordered copies of Ruhnama to be placed in every school and library and mandated that it be read in schools, universities and government offices. Questions on Ruhnama teachings were included as part of the driving test and citizens were ordered to read the Ruhnama every Saturday.

Prospective government employees were tested on the book at job interviews. Turkmenbashy was reported to have said that God himself told him that everyone who has read the book would come directly to heaven. Bookstores and government offices were required to display it prominently and all mosques were to display it as prominently as the *Quran.* If an imam refused this decree, the mosque would be demolished, although with more than 90% of the population in Turkmenistan being Muslim, this was tough to enforce.

He further upset many Muslims when he had the walls of the largest Mosque in Turkmenistan inscribed with verses from both the Quran and the Ruhnama. In August 2005, the first part of the Ruhnama was launched into orbit so that it could "conquer space" as well as the earth.

In 2002, Türkmenbaşy decreed that days of the week and months of the year should be renamed. January was changed to Türkmenbaşy, February renamed Baýdak after the Turkmen Flag, April was changed to Gurbansoltan in his mother's honour. Also in honour of his mother the Turkmen word for bread was changed to Gurbansoltansofswing. September was to be named Ruhnama after his book.

In 2004 men were banned from having a beard and long hair. This rule remains in place although men over 70 are allowed to grow their beard. In 2005 lip-syncing was banned, as was recorded music on TV and car radios were banned. All video games were banned in 2006.

Despite its quirky delights, Turkmenistan is not a popular tourist destination. At about 10,000 per year, Turkmenistan attracts fewer visitors than North Korea.

Back to the Bible -

The Garden of Eden was paradise, a place where the man and his helper could do whatever they liked. Except eat from the tree of knowledge. (God's writers obviously understood from the beginning that an educated flock was much harder to control.)

A talking snake (undoubtedly acting on God's orders - who else was there?) tricked Eve into eating an apple and she tricked Adam into doing the same. Suddenly they both understood that all that fornicating fun they'd been having was now a sin. Which of course did not stop them doing it. Just why God sent the talking snake to trick Eve is a mystery. If he wanted them to remain blissfully ignorant, he wouldn't have done that. But apparently he did want them to understand sin, while pretending he didn't want that.

Having demonstrated his **narcissism**, God now ups his game with perhaps the most vile **dirty trick of all time** topped off with a large dollop of **hypocrisy.**

Then the Lord God said to the woman, "What is this you have done?"

The woman said, "The serpent deceived me, and I ate."

So the Lord God said to the serpent, "Because you have done this,"Cursed are you above all livestock and all wild animals! You will crawl on your belly and you will eat dust all the days of your life. And I will put enmity between you and the woman, and between your offspring and hers; he will crush your head, and you will strike his heel."

So God created a talking snake apparently for the sole purpose of deceiving the woman and then cursed it, and all its future generations to an existence of never ending misery for doing exactly what he created it to do. Exactly the sort of thing a **psychopathic sadist** would do to a captive creature.

To the woman he said,

"I will make your pains in childbearing very severe; with painful labor you will give birth to children. Your desire will

be for your husband, and he will rule over you. "

Taking the opportunity to provide a role model for **psychopathic abusive husbands** everywhere, God shouted, **"Now look what me made me do!"** Well, sort of.

God openly declares right here that he could have designed the human reproductive process to be absolutely painless for women, perhaps by laying a small egg or having a teeny tiny baby like a panda or a kangaroo. But no, because he'd deceived the woman, and she'd reacted exactly how he planned, he now declared that he would make her and every other woman who ever shall live, suffer terrible pain in childbirth.

How was Eve to know that snakes weren't meant to talk? Or that a talking snake might tell lies or try to trick her? If Eve had any knowledge of snakes, or knowledge of con men and lies, she wouldn't have fallen for God's dirty trick, but knowledge was forbidden. How could Adam and Eve understand the concept of sin or dirty tricksters without eating from the tree of knowledge? They never stood a chance. **Thus the first Catch 22 was invented by God**. (Whether his writers did that deliberately is debatable as their story telling skills were not well developed.)

Priests tried to keep the meaning of the Bible hidden behind the Latin language for as long as they could, perhaps because they thought that any woman reading as far as this would rightfully think that God was a lying, cheating asshole who

certainly did not deserve to be respected, obeyed or praised in
any way at all.

*To Adam he said, "Because you listened to your wife and
ate fruit from the tree about which I commanded you, 'You
must not eat from it,'*

*"Cursed is the ground because of you; through painful toil
you will eat food from it all the days of your life. It will
produce thorns and thistles for you, and you will eat the
plants of the field. By the sweat of your brow you will eat your
food until you return to the ground, since from it you were
taken; for dust you are and to dust you will return."*

God's punishment for Adam was almost trivial compared
to the punishment given to all women for all time. The
misogyny was there right from the beginning.

In the NIV (the New International Version of the Bible)
Adam and Eve are referred to as husband and wife, although
whether Eve's wedding dress was white or whether she was
naked for the ceremony there was no mention. Presumably
God conducted the service, or possibly the serpent, as the only
other character with a speaking role in this part of the story,
told Adam he could kiss the bride.

Because they'd used their gift of free will to disobey him,
God ordered them out of the garden and into the wide world
where food was not so plentiful, thus making sure that future
humans would have to work for their food. God decided to
punish all of humanity for all time because two people fell for

a dirty trick that he perpetrated. A dirty trick that they had no chance of avoiding. Without any knowledge of evil they could not possibly have anticipated God's evil plan.

One theme that emerges here is that God's ideal form of punishment is never ending. Or is it his only form of punishment? Priests will give you a pass for a few Hail Marys and a donation, but when God's judgement comes down, it's hellfire for eternity. God seems to be such a horrifically sadistic bastard you might start to wonder if he only invented the concept of the afterlife so that punishment, pain and suffering would never end.

We think of people who kill others as being evil but God doesn't settle for merely killing, he wants those who displease him, aka pretty much everybody, to suffer excruciating pain, forever. **So he's not just a bit of a sadist, he's demonstrably the ultimate psychopathic abuser and super sadist of all time.**

So now Adam and Eve had to wear leaves over their naughty bits because they were ashamed to have been tricked. In fact the Garden of Eden was never actually paradise at all, it was merely the location for God's vile squid game and the beginning of his endless effort to impose suffering and subservience on humanity.

Adam and Eve continued to sin and bore two sons, Cain and Abel. The sons were under close scrutiny by God, who can, allegedly, simultaneously love, know and individually care for billions of people, so his focus on the two boys when there were only four humans in the universe may have felt somewhat intrusive.

Anyway, the lads understood that in addition to praising God on the Sabbath, they had to make offerings to him as well. When God judged Abel's offering to be inferior to Cain's, Cain got jealous and killed Abel. So with only four humans to care for at this time, God was not doing so well at keeping his hamsters alive. Already he'd managed to infuse Adam and Eve with deception and sin and engendered murderous rage and jealousy in Cain. If the omnipotent one had been a bit more hands-off, perhaps none of that crap would have happened.

But it did (allegedly) so God, staying in character, cursed Cain for acting out on the rage God had caused. If God was giving his full attention to these four people (who else was there?) and the result was deadly chaos, it's a minor miracle that the world today is so amazingly peaceful. Relatively speaking.

The faithful are known to claim that humans are God's perfect creation, but a quick glance at the score card indicates that God didn't think so. Of the four original humans, one was murdered by his brother, and of the three humans left, God cursed all of them, conveniently overlooking the fact that all of the supposed sins they had committed were as a result of God's own machinations.

NOT VERY INTELLIGENT DESIGN THREE

Cain went out from the Lord's presence and lived in the land of Nod, east of Eden.

So Cain was able to leave the presence of the omnipresent one, presumably on foot, which implies that omnipresence does not extend beyond walking distance.

Cain made love to his wife, and she became pregnant and gave birth to Enoch.

What?

Where the hell did Cain's wife come from? Even Mitchell and Webb's lazy screenwriters don't make continuity cock-ups of that magnitude.

Anyway…

Cain was then building a city, …

A city? Who the fuck for? At this point one man, his wife (who doesn't seem to be worthy of a name along with most other women in this tome of endless **misogyny**) and baby Enoch (who does get a name to go with his dick) are the only humans anywhere east of Eden, or in fact anywhere other than Eden, where Cain's mum and dad and God are. Presumably Cain's wife's mum and dad must be somewhere north, west or south of Eden, or perhaps they exist outside of space and time.

… and he named it after his son Enoch. To Enoch was born Irad, and Irad was the father of Mehujael, and Mehujael was the father of Methushael, and Methushael was the father of

Lamech.

We can assume that some women were involved but why waste time mentioning them? Wait on…

Lamech married two women, one named Adah and the other Zillah.

Bigamy is introduced here as a concept and apparently it's totally fine. Lamech married both women so it wasn't adultery. Whether Adah or Zillah took another husband or two is not mentioned, but that would have probably been fine too. Kidding. That would have surely been punished with some form of eternal torture, following stoning to death.

Adah gave birth to Jabal; he was the father of those who live in tents and raise livestock. His brother's name was Jubal; he was the father of all who play stringed instruments and pipes. Zillah also had a son, Tubal-Cain, who forged all kinds of tools out of bronze and iron. Tubal-Cain's sister was Naamah.

Lamech said to his wives,

"Adah and Zillah, listen to me; wives of Lamech, hear my words. I have killed a man for wounding me, a young man for injuring me. If Cain is avenged seven times, then Lamech seventy-seven times."

Well that just seemed to pop in out of nowhere. Will we hear more about this unusually detailed incident later on? Perhaps. Perhaps not. Who cares?

Adam made love to his wife again, and she gave birth to a son and named him Seth, saying, "God has granted me another child in place of Abel, since Cain killed him."

Adam's wife has apparently become totally submissive to God, thanking him for another painful childbirth and harbouring no animosity to him for causing the death of Abel.

Seth also had a son, and he named him Enosh.

At that time people began to call on the name of the Lord.

"Dear God, make it stop!" they called. "Enough of the boring list of names shit."

Anyone still awake after all that nonsense?

It's hard to say if the birth of Seth is meant to be a flashback, but I suppose it must be, because if you follow the above, then Lamech is the great, great, great, great grandson of Adam and Eve. Then again maybe it's contemporaneous, because we're about to embark on a boring and repetitive recitation of the names of men who live for more than 900 years and have a succession of children. What's the point of saying they all lived so long? Mysterious.

Genesis 5   From Adam to Noah

This is the written account of Adam's family line.

Reading this part of Genesis is like being at a party where you get stuck with one of those people who talk and talk and all they tell you are facts and figures about people you've either never heard of and/or really don't care about, like one of those verbal family news roundup Christmas card/letter things that were a bit of a fad for a while.

Like a crazed **megalomaniac**, with **no hint of self-awareness**, God persisted in his wilful campaign of death and destruction. Somehow Adam and his remaining two sons manage to produce generations of humans, presumably with poor old Eve enduring a whole lot more deliberately inflicted suffering in childbirth but the shortage of human stock to avoid inbreeding problems are mysteriously glossed over in the official account.

We can forgive God's writers for their lack of knowledge of the universe, but the fundamentals of reproduction should have been fairly well known by then, and could have been easily accommodated by less lazy writers. Meaning a few daughters for Eve at the very least. Even ancient farmers would understand that a single female was not an efficient way to generate a large flock.

Anyway, fast forward through generations of humans, all of whom God then adjudges to be evil, so evil in fact that they need to be wiped out. All except for the single good one.

It's worth pausing just a moment to reflect on the supposedly infinite power, wisdom and loving kindness of a God who creates his masterpiece, the human race, in his own image, and then decides it disgusts him so much that he must kill it all.

A form of self-loathing perhaps? Severe remorse and regret at the very least.

We all know that superheroes and supervillains have limits to their powers and God appears to be no different in this regard. Instead of snapping his fingers or waving a wand, God decides to drown everybody for their wicked ways.

Imagine a first time Bible reader getting this far into it, nodding their head and going, yeah, I buy all this, yep, makes sense, nothing implausible so far. Ya think? You can see why it requires childhood indoctrination and salesmen in fancy robes using scare tactics to sell this nonsense.

Where were we?

God, who deliberately inflicted sin on humanity in the Garden of Eden, now decides he doesn't like sin, or human beings in general, and will therefore become the ultimate **misanthropic sociopath** by killing everybody.

*The Lord regretted that he had made human beings on the earth, and **his heart was deeply troubled**.*

So the Lord said, "I will wipe from the face of the earth the human race I have created—and with them the animals, the birds and the creatures that move along the ground—for I regret that I have made them."

But Noah found favor in the eyes of the Lord.

He instructs Noah, the only good man on earth, to build a vessel large enough to carry breeding pairs of every species on earth. At this point it's apparent that the writers had no idea just how many species existed on earth, and how far away some of them lived. If they'd known about polar bears and penguins, they would have had to rethink the whole stupid story. But God didn't bother to let his writers know about any inconvenient facts as he apparently wasn't expecting this story to last long enough to be read by people who would instantly recognise its stupidity.

God makes it rain and rain and rain, and all the animals sing songs and have a jolly good time and none of them eat each other, and there are no sanitation issues, and there's enough room for everybody, and after forty days they all get off and the penguins wave goodbye to the polar bears never to see them again. How they all found their way home is a mystery, as it would be thousands of years before humans learnt to navigate over such distances.

It's unclear just how many men, women and children drowned during the course of the great flood, but who cares as God loved each and every one of them unconditionally. Except he didn't. He regretted that every single one of them was born. He said they were all sinners, who are to this day, and beyond, presumably burning in the fires of hell. Nice work, God. Bloody **psychopath**.

After the flood, God made a rainbow to celebrate his promise (presumably to Noah and family as there's nobody else left alive) not to kill everybody again, apparently once more feeling **remorse and self-doubt** for his actions. He

regretted making them all sinners and then he **regretted killing them all.** He had enough crazy going on in there to keep an army of psychiatrists busy.

So Noah came out, together with his sons and his wife and his sons' wives.

All the animals and all the creatures that move along the ground and all the birds—everything that moves on land— came out of the ark, one kind after another.

Then Noah built an altar to the Lord and, taking some of all the clean animals and clean birds, he sacrificed burnt offerings on it.

Had these "clean" animals and "clean" birds reproduced while on the ark? If not then Noah's sacrifice of them was an act of extermination of those species. Also why did God create "clean animals" and "dirty" animals? Did he regret making the "dirty" ones?

The Lord smelled the pleasing aroma and said in his heart: "Never again will I curse the ground because of humans, even though every inclination of the human heart is evil from childhood. And never again will I destroy all living creatures, as I have done.

In addition to the smell of burning bodies, God would also come to love the smell of napalm in the morning, as evidenced by the never-ending series of wars his perfect creations would undertake.

The Table of Nations

The Table of Nations is another excruciatingly boring recitation of names of people. What was its purpose? To lend an air of authenticity? To appear to be an official record of actual events perhaps?

In an era before simple cut and paste was possible, the lazy writers still executed a version of it.

The best part about this list of names is their similarity to the sort of names that children make up when they have imaginary friends. Here are some imaginary children's names I found on the internet. Marjil and Parjil, Macky, Kacky, Stribble, Ronjon, Inchog, Clunga, Ho, Bubblegum, Merdy, Sabi, Alish, Baataba, the boy the girl and Lindsey, The Poonatanna Man, Eelik, Wahneu, Peekin, Rosen, Nina, and Refgok.

Feel free to skip forward to the end of this section when you tire of it. It is only quoted here to illustrate the mind numbing stupidity of the thing.

This is the account of Shem, Ham and Japheth, Noah's sons, who themselves had sons after the flood.

Once again the females don't even get a mention. The full-blown **misogyny** of the God of the Abrahamic religions was solidified on every page.

The Japhethites

The sons of Japheth:

Gomer, Magog, Madai, Javan, Tubal, Meshek and Tiras.

The sons of Gomer:

Ashkenaz, Riphath and Togarmah.

The sons of Javan:

Elishah, Tarshish, the Kittites and the Rodanites. (From these the maritime peoples spread out into their territories by their clans within their nations, each with its own language.)

The Hamites

The sons of Ham:

Cush, Egypt, Put and Canaan.

The sons of Cush:

Seba, Havilah, Sabtah, Raamah and Sabteka.

The sons of Raamah:

Sheba and Dedan.

Cush was the father of Nimrod, who became a mighty warrior on the earth.

He was a mighty hunter before the Lord; that is why it is said, "Like Nimrod, a mighty hunter before the Lord."

This crap is a lot less painful to endure if you imagine David Mitchell or Rowan Atkinson reading it aloud.

The first centers of his kingdom were Babylon, Uruk, Akkad and Kalneh, in Shinar. From that land he went to Assyria, where he built Nineveh, Rehoboth Ir, Calah and Resen, which is between Nineveh and Calah—which is the great city.

Egypt was the father of

the Ludites, Anamites, Lehabites, Naphtuhites, Pathrusites, Kasluhites (from whom the Philistines came) and Caphtorites.

Canaan was the father of

Sidon his firstborn, and of the Hittites, Jebusites, Amorites, Gigashites, Hivites, Arkites, Sinites, Arvadites, Zemarites and Hamathites.

Later the Canaanite clans scattered and the borders of Canaan reached from Sidon toward Gerar as far as Gaza, and then toward Sodom, Gomorrah, Admah and Zeboyim, as far as Lasha.

These are the sons of Ham by their clans and languages, in their territories and nations.

The Semites

Sons were also born to Shem, whose older brother was Japheth; Shem was the ancestor of all the sons of Eber.

The sons of Shem:

Elam, Ashur, Arphaxad, Lud and Aram.

The sons of Aram:

Uz, Hul, Gether and Meshek.

Arphaxad was the father of Shelah,

and Shelah the father of Eber.

Two sons were born to Eber:

One was named Peleg, because in his time the earth was divided; his brother was named Joktan.

Not sure why Peleg was singled out for an explanation of his name. Also if that was the reason, why wasn't everybody in the time the earth was divided (whatever the fuck that means) named Peleg? His brother was named Joktan because of his fondness for lying under the noonday sun with no pants on.

Joktan was the father of

Almodad, Sheleph, Hazarmaveth, Jerah, Hadoram, Uzal, Diklah, Obal, Abimael, Sheba, Ophir, Havilah and Jobab. All these were sons of Joktan.

The region where they lived stretched from Mesha toward Sephar, in the eastern hill country.

These are the sons of Shem by their clans and languages, in their territories and nations.

These are the clans of Noah's sons, according to their lines of descent, within their nations. From these the nations spread out over the earth after the flood.

Footnotes

Genesis 10:2 Sons may mean descendants or

successors or nations; also in verses 3, 4, 6, 7, 20-23, 29 and 31.

Genesis 10:8   Father may mean ancestor or predecessor or founder;

Just in case anyone had any misgivings about the accuracy of all this, sons might mean nations, one might mean a million.

Genesis 11   The Tower of Babel

Now the whole world had one language and a common speech. As people moved eastward, they found a plain in Shinar and settled there.

They said to each other, "Come, let's make bricks and bake them thoroughly." They used brick instead of stone, and tar for mortar. Then they said, "Come, let us build ourselves a city, with a tower that reaches to the heavens, so that we may make a name for ourselves; otherwise we will be scattered over the face of the whole earth."

But the Lord came down to see the city and the tower the people were building. The Lord said, "If as one people speaking the same language they have begun to do this, then nothing they plan to do will be impossible for them. Come, let us go down and confuse their language so they will not understand each other."

So the Lord scattered them from there over all the earth, and they stopped building the city. That is why it was called

Babel—because there the Lord confused the language of the whole world. From there the Lord scattered them over the face of the whole earth.

Here God is yet again **dissatisfied** with the creatures he has created. This time he disapproves of humans showing intelligence and peaceful co-operation with one another. God's preference for humanity was clearly for something other than that, something more along the lines of stupidity and tribal conflict. As time goes on this seems to be one of his greatest successes as different religious tribes ceaselessly endeavour to kill one another.

It's lucky that God, whilst euphorically inhaling the burnt offerings of Noah, vowed to "never again destroy all living creatures" because he was apparently grumpy enough, once again, to kill a large number. Genocide 2, Babel : The Second Great Cleansing.

God has thus far expressed no desire for humans to be anything other than his subservient sheep, and he does not hesitate to behave in the manner of a boot stamping on a human face - forever.

From Shem to Abram

This is the account of Shem's family line.

In which Shem begets some sons and baguettes some daughters, but no daughter worthy of a name.

Two years after the flood, when Shem was 100 years old, he became the father of Arphaxad. And after he became the father of Arphaxad, Shem lived 500 years and had other sons and daughters.

When Arphaxad had lived 35 years, he became the father of Shelah. And after he became the father of Shelah, Arphaxad lived 403 years and had other sons and daughters, including Anthrax and Oxycontin.

When Shelah had lived 30 years, he became the father of Eber. And after he became the father of Eber, Shelah lived 403 years and had other sons and daughters, including Ebola and Nigel.

When Eber had lived 34 years, he became the father of Peleg. And after he became the father of Peleg, Eber lived 430 years and had other sons and daughters, including Tchundah and Windypop.

When Peleg had lived 30 years, he became the father of Reu. And after he became the father of Reu, Peleg lived 209 years and had other sons and daughters, including Blackbeard and Pegleg Pete.

When Reu had lived 32 years, he became the father of Serug. And after he became the father of Serug, Reu lived 207 years and had other sons and daughters, including Bam Bam, Wilma, Barney and Fred.

When Serug had lived 30 years, he became the father of Nahor. And after he became the father of Nahor, Serug lived

200 years and had other sons and daughters.

When Nahor had lived 29 years, he became the father of Terah. And after he became the father of Terah, Nahor lived 119 years and had other sons and daughters.

After Terah had lived 70 years, he became the father of Abram, Nahor and Haran.

God chose Abram to be "the father of many nations." Abram changed his name to Abraham, and God promised him the land of Canaan (Israel) forever. As a sign of this promise, the sons of Abraham are circumcised. God tested Abraham's loyalty by asking him to kill his son Isaac.

That God, eh? What a character. It's like he'd always ask himself, what would an absolute bastard do? And then he'd think of something worse.

Abraham was ready to do it, but God sent an angel to stop him. God told him there would be no more human sacrifice.

Animal sacrifice was apparently still fine. Nothing like that aroma of burnt offerings in the morning.

God eventually sacrificed his own son, but that didn't count because… reasons of the mysterious kind. And scapegoating was still a pretty normal activity back then.

God destroyed the evil cities of Sodom and Gomorrah, saving only Abraham's nephew Lot and his daughters.

God sure does seem to enjoy a spot of genocide. Did God's remorse include regretting his vow never to commit mass murder again, or did he just regret the mass murder each and every time he did it?

A lovely sequence of pantomime-style storytelling ensues.

Isaac and his wife Rebekah had two twin sons, Esau and Jacob. Jacob traded food to Esau for Esau's right to carry the family name. Rebekah helped trick Isaac, who was old and blind, into giving his final blessing to Jacob by dressing him in fur (Isaac felt Jacob's furs and thought he was his hairy twin, Esau). Esau later got a blessing of his own.

Jacob left to find a wife. He found Rachel and worked for her father, Lavan, for seven years to marry her, but was tricked into marrying her sister Leah. He worked for another seven years to marry Rachel. He went back to his home, then moved to Bethel, where God told him to change his name to Israel. Jacob later also marries the servants of Leah and Rachel, whose names are Bilah and Zilpah.

God was very hands-on at this time. When did he get sick of personally manipulating us? Did he ever get sick of killing us?

Jacob had twelve sons named Reuben, Simeon, Levi, Judah, Issaschar, Zebulun, Gad, Dan, Asher, Naftali, Joseph, and Benjamin. His wife Rachel died after she gave birth to Benjamin.

Jacob gave his son Joseph a coat of many colors. Joseph's brothers were jealous, so they sold him into slavery in Egypt. They covered his coat in blood and told their father he had died.

Who would sell their brother into slavery because they were jealous of a coat? And then destroy the coat? Why not just destroy the coat? Were they getting advice from God?

Joseph became a great leader in Egypt by predicting a long famine by explaining the pharaoh's dreams. During the famine, his brothers came to Egypt to buy food. They did not know that Joseph was the leader. Joseph first tricked the brothers, but then gave them food and let them stay in Goshen in Egypt.

Jacob blessed his sons and then died.

And that's more than enough of that nonsense.

Even though this section is long and repetitive it's just a tiny portion of the Bible, yet it does illustrate just how often the God of the Bible exhibits human characteristics.

He was a con man and grifter right from the start with the "talking snake and tree of knowledge of good and evil" scam. Then he provided a role model for psychopathic abusive husbands everywhere, with his "Now look what me made me do" abuse of Eve, blaming her for things that he caused her to do.

Misogyny pokes its head up repeatedly throughout, indicating the writer/s were male and therefore human. He regretted making all humans sinners and then he regretted killing them all, and felt remorse and self-loathing every time he killed some more.

For a god created by the human brain, that's a pretty good villain by any standards, wracked by all manner of human emotions. One would think that a real God would be above such feelings.

The Ten Commandments

The Ten Commandments appear in the book of Deuteronomy. The Book of Deuteronomy (literally "second law" from Greek deuteros + nomos) is the fifth book of the Jewish Torah, where it is called Devarim (Hebrew: דְּבָרִים), "the words [of Moses]", and the fifth book of the Christian Old Testament, where it is also known as the Fifth Book of Moses.

There's a lot of cut and paste when it comes to the Abrahamic religions. They share the early stuff, and so they basically come from the same place, both geographically and ideologically, but somehow, from that first book that contained the ten commandments they're all based on, religious believers have found reasons to not only disagree, but disagree to the point where Jews, Christians, Sunni, Shia and many, many offshoots have found it imperative to disagree, hate and kill each other ever since.

Nice work, God. How come you didn't see that coming, Mr Omniscient? Or was that the plan you evil bastard? However you look at them, the ten commandments have proved to be a pretty ineffectual piece of work from the one god to rule them all.

When a ruler with absolute power decrees the ten most important rules, or laws, for his subjects to live by, it is reasonable to deduce that these rules not only indicate what that ruler thinks are the most important things, but also very clearly indicate the sort of mind that thought they were the most important things.

The first four of these things according to the God of the Bible are really just one thing - the requirement for absolute devotional servitude to the ruler.

If God is in fact a creation of mankind, a figurehead in front of a curtain, the first four commandments are a clear indication of the intentions of those behind the curtain. Total control.

The following italicised excerpts are from Deuteronomy 5 in the Modern English Version of the Bible, which is an English translation of the Bible begun in 2005 and completed in 2014. The work was edited by James F. Linzey, and is an update of the King James Version, re-translated from the Masoretic Text and the Textus Receptus.

In other words the Bible has been in a constant state of evolution ever since the very first version, which is an annoying and inconvenient truth for deniers of the concept of evolution.

Then Moses called all Israel and said to them:

The Lord talked with you face to face on the mountain from the midst of the fire. I stood between the Lord and you at that time to declare to you the word of the Lord; for you were afraid because of the fire and would not go up to the mountain. He said:

Notice that God himself never appears before large groups of people. He always passes on his message through individual charlatans and liars oops I mean messengers. He could solve all doubt as to his existence if he weren't so shy. But anyway…

Commandment No 1

I am the Lord, your God, … You shall have no other gods before Me.

That's fairly definitive. **Narcissism** 101, Chapter 1, Verse 1.

Okay then, we hear where you're coming from, now on to the the list of the most absolutely important rules for humanity to live by.

Commandment No 2

You shall not make yourself any graven image, or any likeness of anything that is in heaven above, or that is in the earth beneath, or that is in the waters beneath the earth; you shall not bow down to them, nor serve them. For I, the Lord your God, am a jealous God, visiting the iniquity of the fathers on the children, and on the third and fourth generations of those who hate Me, but showing mercy to thousands of them that love Me and keep My commandments.

Okay, so God's a **jealous** guy (totally consistent with the

NOT VERY INTELLIGENT DESIGN THREE

narcissism) and if we don't obey his rules he will punish not just those who disobey, but the next four generations as well. That's way more **violent** than most mob bosses who don't kill more than your immediate family. Unless you've really pissed them off. This God father figure will slaughter four generations just for making him jealous. For carving a statue of him? A touch **psychotic** perhaps? God is the numero uno and mankind must obey orders.

Right. Got it. So, what are the rules to live by?

Commandment No 3

You shall not take the name of the Lord your God in vain, for the Lord will not exonerate anyone who takes His name in vain.

Holy shit! Are there any rules that aren't just about praising you, you **narcissistic** fuck? And what's that? No exoneration?

If your toast lands face down and you say something like, Jesus Fucking Christ, or God Dammit, you will never be forgiven, ever, even if you pray to God every day for the rest of your life. It says it right there in the commandment itself - *the Lord will not exonerate anyone who takes His name in vain.* **No forgiveness** for blasphemy. No second chances. A bit harsh? (When you read this stuff you quickly begin to understand where the fundamentalists get their crazy ideas from.)

Commandment No 4

Keep the Sabbath day, to keep it holy, just as the Lord your God has commanded you. Six days you shall labor and do all your work, but the seventh day is the Sabbath of the Lord your God. On it you shall not do any work: you, nor your son, nor your daughter, nor your male servant, nor your female servant, nor your ox, nor your donkey, nor any of your livestock, nor the foreigner that is within your gates...

Aaaand... the fourth most important rule is also about praising you.

Just one day a week? So modest not to demand three or four days dedicated to praising the most holy one. (Also worth noting that "servant" almost certainly means **slave**, but that translation has evolved.)

Commandment No 5

Honor your father and your mother, just as the Lord your God has commanded you, that your days may be prolonged, and that it may go well with you in the land which the Lord your God is giving you.

At last, the **narcissist** gives the **narcissism** a rest.

But this rule's almost as shitty as the first four because the children of good parents love and respect them without needing to be commanded, and commanding children to honour parents who have abused or betrayed them is just depraved.

Plus it's another one about servitude. Even if your parents

sold you as a sex slave at the age of five you must honour them. What a brilliantly useless rule to round out the top 5 most important rules about everything. Jesus wept. Whoops that's blasphemy. One way ticket to Hell.

Commandment No 6

You shall not murder.

Solid, even if fairly obvious.

Can't argue with that one.

Commandment No 7

You shall not commit adultery.

But men can have multiple wives, including really really young ones (children). And they can have sex slaves as well. As written, it's not specifically **misogynistic**, but in context it absolutely is. It's a rule that was really meant to apply only to women.

Commandment No 8

You shall not steal.

Solid. Good rule.

Commandment No 9

You shall not bear false witness against your neighbor.

Solid. Probably the most valuable one of all. Theft and murder are wrong, but that's so obvious that everyone knows it instinctually. Telling lies about other people can be just as damaging though, and is a very worthy commandment.

Commandment No 10

You shall not covet your neighbor's wife, nor shall you covet your neighbor's house, his field, his male servant, his female servant, his ox, his donkey, or anything that belongs to your neighbor.

And just when the rules were getting sensible, God rounds off the top ten with a thought crime. Possibly to remind people that he can read their minds.

We have no control over what we think. Making thoughts a crime is the work of a **psychotic sadist**.

Besides, provided we don't in any way act on our admiration of our neighbour's property, what harm is done? This one is just another way to control and oppress, to keep the boot on the face.

Having made the human mind susceptible to jumping all over the place and having random thoughts popping in, the big bad **control freak** will now command you not to do things your are utterly powerless not to do. What a prick!

These are the words the Lord spoke to all your assembly at the mountain out from the midst of the fire, the cloud, and the thick darkness with a great voice, and He added no more. He wrote them on two tablets of stone and gave them to me.

And there they are. The most quoted, most revered set of rules in human history. Yet all it takes is a moment's scrutiny to reveal that six of them are a complete load of shit, two are correct and obvious, one needs work, and just one of them has any sort of depth.

Which raises the question, what commandments should have been there in place of all the narcissism and psychotic hellfire? There are seven slots available. Seven spaces for some directives for humanity that the God of the Bible thought were not worth mentioning. Without trying to write them all out as full commandments, a list of topics should serve to illustrate the moral depravity of God's writers, who thought the following things weren't important enough to include -

Rape

Slavery

Bigotry and discrimination

Child abuse, whether physical, sexual or mental, such as the religious indoctrination of children with threats of eternal torture

Violence, all forms, mental and physical, from personal assault to all-out war

Animal cruelty

Hypocrisy

Freedom of belief and freedom from belief

Political corruption

I'm sure there are more things that should be on this list, but seeing the sort of things God didn't think were worth mentioning may to some extent explain the behaviour of many evangelical and extremist members of God's army.

God has always made himself elusive and invisible. Given that he devoted the first four commandments to the concept of praising him (with threats of extreme punishment for disobedience), why hide his message from most of the planet? Why restrict personal appearances to cloud formations, damp stained walls and pieces of toast? Why hide behind individual messengers and prophets when he could light up the whole sky and reveal himself in all his fiery, jealous, genocidal glory?

Is it because he works in mysterious ways or is it that he's incapable of doing anything like that because he only exists in the imagination of the human brain?

Thankfully the latter, because such a mean-spirited, capricious asshole could easily look at the Christian fondness for the crucifix (which absolutely complies with the dictionary definition of a graven image), and send every Catholic to burn in hell forever. Even if your grandfather renounced Catholicism, and you and your parents never set foot in a church, you and your children are still going to hell

under the third and fourth generation rule of Commandment
number 2.

The Form of God

What does God look like?

According to Genesis, God created mankind in his own image. Unsurprisingly therefore, God does indeed look like one of us in most of the art funded by wealthy Christians. Specifically he looks like an old white man with long hair and a beard.

But why would God look like that? He doesn't live here on earth. He's never been subjected to earth's gravity or atmosphere. Apart from that time he turned a third of himself into a human embryo and then spent thirty odd years here, doing surprisingly little considering he was the creator of the whole universe. (Jesus' visit to earth was like if you went to a big music festival where the headliner was billed as the greatest rock and roll act that the world had ever seen, but when you finally found him, he was a hippy sitting in the woods out behind the campground playing a ukulele, with twelve fans sitting cross legged in front of him.)

According to science, the reason we look like we do is because we evolved to survive and function in the environment of the planet we evolved on. We evolved to eat the food, drink the water and breath the atmosphere of planet Earth. We developed bones and muscles to overcome the force of gravity that would otherwise keep us stuck to the ground like rocks and shopping malls.

When creatures get big and heavy, like elephants, their own weight stops them moving or changing direction as easily as we do. Try as they might, even the lithest elephants will never win any medals for rhythmic gymnastics or synchronised swimming. The biggest dinosaurs were probably getting close to the maximum size limit for mobile creatures on a planet of this size. In fact they proved to be too big in the end because they couldn't run fast enough to get out of the way of the big asteroid.

Not only do we look like we do because of where we evolved, we only continue to look like we do, because we continue to live here. We now know that astronauts' bodies start to change as soon as they leave planet earth. Without the earth's atmosphere, pressure and gravity we start to change. The changes are measurable in individuals after mere months in space. Who knows what we'd look like after an expedition to deep space that lasted many generations.

If God doesn't live on a planet that's exactly like earth there's no reason for him to look anything like us. If he lives in space above the clouds where there's no air or food, he wouldn't need a mouth or an anus. He wouldn't need feet or legs to move around. Or fingers to pick his nose with, because he wouldn't have a nose. If you live in zero gravity you don't need bones to stop your body collapsing into a pile of jello. Though you wouldn't be a pile of jello in a weightless environment, you'd be a floating blob. A bit like a ghost.

When God speaks to his faithful they hear him inside their brains. Is that because that's where he lives? Either way, he doesn't use his mouth for speaking so it must be there for for eating. What's the food like in heaven? Is God a carnivore? Probably. He loves the smell of burning flesh according to Genesis, and he's not averse to a spot of slaughter. God didn't need opposable thumbs to create the universe, so why does he have them at all? Is the reason he has long hair and a beard because there are no hairdressers in heaven? Okay so this is dissolving into absurdity now, but I blame that on the subject matter. And the third glass of Merlot.

If God looks like the old man on the ceiling of the Sistine Chapel, is that because he made us in his image, or because we made him in our image? He would not look like that if he lived either in space or outside of time and space. In fact there are only two places where he would look like that. On earth, and nobody claims that he lives there, or in the imagination of mankind.

Moving on.

A Vision of God

In 2014, Larry Person saw that a Catholic Archdiocese had listed a former orphanage for sale. Larry wouldn't have paid any attention to the news in the local paper if he hadn't recently encountered an old school friend who told him that he'd made a lot of money from boarding houses. The heft and sparkle of Corey Turner's wristwatch and the fist-sized Bentley key fob on the bar next to his martini made Larry think that Corey Turner had done very well for himself.

When Larry questioned the ability of boarding house tenants to pay their rent on a regular basis Turner said the secret was to only have tenants that were prepared to have their welfare cheques paid into an account controlled by the boarding house.

"Is that legal?" asked Larry.

"Not, strictly," said Turner, "but what are they gonna do? Poor people get fucked over all the time. They're used to it."

Congregations in Christian churches have waned in recent years in many parts of the western world. Accordingly, churches and other church properties are sold when they can no longer draw sufficient donors to remain profitable. Or sometimes for other reasons.

St John's Guiding Light For Boys Catholic School and

Orphanage wasn't for sale on account of a diminishing congregation. Partly it was for sale because the school and orphanage had been closed down for many years, but mostly the Archdiocese of St John's was selling the property to pay the fees of a very aggressive lawyer who had sued them into submission on behalf of former students and residents, most of whom had survived a systemic onslaught of physical and sexual abuse during the nineteen fifties and sixties. Because of the reputation of the property, the price was low, as prospective purchasers calculated the land minus demolition costs as being the true value.

Although he hadn't done as well as his old school friend, Larry did own a substantial house as well as a block of four cheap apartments. Thus he had sufficient collateral to purchase the three level, forty-eight room crime scene and a quick calculation of the value of a hundred or more welfare checks every week meant the property seemed like a potential gold mine.

The impending auction date left Larry with no time to do proper due diligence either on the building or on his own finances, so when the hammer fell he was happy that his winning bid was a little less than he'd been prepared to pay. He smiled as he imagined his new extra large wristwatch and big, shiny key fob.

Larry's dream was replaced by reality when it became apparent that the costs associated with bringing the old torture house up to the standard required for the granting of permits to operate as a boarding house were massive, leaving Larry a long way shy of the necessary liquidity.

His calls to Corey Turner seeking advice, and hopefully investment funds, went unanswered and unreturned. He offered a partnership to a builder he knew, on the basis that the builder would do the necessary refurbishment and they would share the proceeds.

Ken Carpenter accompanied Larry on an inspection of the building. In one rather dank and fowl smelling basement room, Ken was stunned to see what appeared in the beam of his flashlight.

"Holy Jesus," he said.

"What?" said Larry.

"Look. Doesn't that look like Jesus to you?"

"Well…" If he applied a little imagination Larry could imagine he saw something resembling Jesus at least as clearly as images sometimes found on pieces of toast.

"People are gonna want to see this."

"Really? Who?"

"All sorts of people."

When Ken called Larry to give him the estimate of what the cost of the renovations might be, Larry was speechless. He managed to say, "Thanks, I'll call you back later," as he ended the call.

"Holy Jesus," he said involuntarily. Which reminded him of Ken's reaction to the wall stain in the basement. Ken said religious people would want to see it. If Larry charged an admission fee, who knows how much he might raise.

Larry called the local newspaper. A reporter came and took photos and Larry was pleasantly surprised to see them on the front page. He shouldn't have been. In the last year things that had made the front page of the local rag included cats in trees, trees being cut down, plans for a new footpath, potholes and a warning about strangers in public toilets.

The photos also made the front page of the online edition where the story was picked up and tweeted by an amused local. Then, much to the delight of Larry, it went viral. Larry was interviewed outside the building by a local TV reporter, during which he referred to the mark on the basement wall as a "Vision of God." He described the atmosphere in the room as having "a physically discernible vibe, as if the Lord himself were present." Larry was not about to let this opportunity for financial redemption slip through his fingers. He ended by encouraging people to come and see for themselves for "a small donation, a tiny fraction of the cost of a journey to Lourdes or to see the Shroud of Turin."

People immediately started turning up to see the apparition for themselves. Larry hired security to fence the property and set up a desk in the entry hall to take money from the curious and the gullible.

An online debate broke out as to whether the apparition was a "Vision of God" or an image of Jesus. Larry had used the term "vision of God" on TV but the thing he was referring to was an image rather than a vision, and many argued that the shape on the wall did seem to be more like a classic Jesus or Mary image rather than a classic God one. Larry came to understand that apparitions of the Virgin Mary were the most popular apparition, followed by those of Jesus, then God, with the Holy Ghost barely registering. Probably because nobody has any idea what the Holy Ghost might look like and what the hell does he do anyway?

It was too big a leap to change the marketing to a Virgin Mary theme, so Larry settled on the moniker, "A Vision of Jesus" when he realised that more people would be inclined to travel and pay to see a miracle of the reappearance of Jesus than of God. Larry had Ken Carpenter do a bit of basic refurbishment to a room off the entry hall and stocked it with AVOJ merchandise.

Business was going well. It wasn't as lucrative as a boarding house would be, but it was enough to take care of Larry's short term cashflow predicament.

When Larry heard of a story that Jesus had returned in the form of an orphan who was at the school in the nineteen sixties he tried to capitalise on it by asking the public to submit photographs of former residents to the AVOJ website.

Larry had initially thought he'd need to limit the time visitors could spend in the basement room with the Vision of Jesus but that turned out to be unnecessary as the odour of mould and stale urine meant that most people could only stand it for a minute or so and once a visitor left the basement the one-way exit was through the gift shop so any visitors wanting to revisit the shrine would need to buy another ticket.

Some skeptics referred to Larry's shrine as the Shroud of Urine and the Apparition of Micturition.

Max Pressaro, the local journalist who first reported on the story, was a little disappointed to have gained no benefit from his work. In an attempt to inject himself back into the story for some possible fame or fortune he decided to conduct a DNA test on a scraping of damp plaster taken from the base of the image.

With the help of his friendly local Police Sergeant, Pressaro had the DNA run through the national database. To his surprise and delight the Sergeant called him to say they had a hit. While there were traces of many different strands of DNA in the scraping provided there was only a big enough sample of one to obtain a match. Not just a hit, an exact match. Even better, they knew exactly where the person could be found. Because that person was in prison.

When Pressaro saw the mugshot he thought he could see a resemblance to the traditional depictions of Jesus, although perhaps there was a little more Charles Manson around the eyes.

Pressaro sprang into action. He arranged for a visit to interview the inmate and wrote a teaser piece about having identified DNA from the Vision of Jesus. Pressaro reported that there was a possibility he was about to meet the reincarnated Jesus rumoured to have been a resident of St Johns in the nineteen sixties. The fact that the man was in prison was seen as a positive. Hadn't Jesus been incarcerated by the authorities on his first visit to planet earth?

At this point things went super viral. Larry needed more staff at A Vision of Jesus, and queues stretched for up to three blocks. The admission price to the basement room went from 10 bucks to 20 to 49.99.

Pressaro had not released the identity of the DNA match, but when he travelled to the prison he was tailed by four news vans and a few cars. Max Pressaro didn't care. He'd go in, interview the new Jesus, post an initial report on his website then come outside to be interviewed by the various gathered networks.

He didn't reveal much, though he did confirm that the inmate had indeed lived at the orphanage and he had been regularly abused and spent many days and weeks in the dungeon, as it was called by the boys at the time. Sometimes he was alone in the dungeon, sometimes there were two or three boys down there at the same time. The abuse and raping didn't happen in the dungeon, that took place upstairs in the offices and rooms of the priests.

One thing that Max didn't reveal, either to the the the TV crews or on his website, was that the new Jesus was serving a very long sentence for a multitude of crimes including crimes of violence and sexual abuse of minors. The judge did express his sympathy and understanding that the horrible abuse and suffering endured by the accused had undoubtedly contributed significantly to his mental pathology, but that such severe crimes simply could not go unpunished. When asked if he had anything to say prior to the judge passing sentence, the accused had said, "What about the priests? They did much worse stuff than I ever did. None of them went to prison."

Max thought that knowledge of the criminal record of the new Jesus would dull the excitement too much. Even though there'd be plenty of sympathy, most people would see it the same way as the judge. Although this was bound to be revealed within a few days if not hours, it was enough time to direct people to his own website where he would hold a YouTube live stream in two hours time in which the big revelation about the origin of the Vision of Jesus and the identity of the new Jesus would be made public.

Max drove away from the prison hoping that the guards wouldn't reveal to the press who he'd just visited. He knew immediately that was naive but he'd given the world the details about his livestream on YouTube, so he should get a big audience.

The story Pressaro told on his livestream was of young boys locked in a basement with no plumbing facilities. Being young boys with no place to pee except for the walls, their punishment time was turned into entertainment by means of a pissing competition. Highest up the wall wins. After a few arguments about the relative heights of the wet areas it was resolved that each attempt had to be made at exactly the same place which made it easy to tell whether the new stream was higher than the old one. After a few years the stain became permanent with every new layer adding to the resemblance to a holy apparition.

A month after Pressaro's livestream, the Vision of Jesus attraction closed its doors for the last time. Larry put the property back on the market and managed to sell it for a price that allowed him to keep his house, although he did lose his block of flats, something that would have been unnecessary but for the massive order of AVOJ Gift Shop merchandise including cups, caps, towels, t-shirts and leather jackets that had been placed by Larry just before the Max Pressaro fiasco.

Max had no follow up story with which to capitalise on his Vision of Jesus scoop, so his moment of fame lasted for just seventeen minutes. His fame diminished even further when he was made redundant from his local newspaper job three months later.

The new owner of St John's wasted no time in demolishing

the building and thus the scene of so much exploitation and abuse was no longer a potential location for the exploitation of the poor, whether young or old.

People may wonder whether the piss on the wall Vision Of Jesus story was the inspiration for the famous work of art known as Piss Christ, but for those paying attention it should be obvious that this story is a work of fiction written some years after the creation of the famous Piss Christ artwork. It was also written many years after it supposedly occurred and there are no known contemporaneous records of any part of it. Something it has in common with the Bible.

The Character of God

If God were a man, would he be a man of good character?

Not if you recall the earlier discussion of a person of good character as being someone who would not shag a friend's wife, because God did shag another bloke's wife. Although he wasn't actually a friend and she was supposedly still a virgin despite her pregnancy, so who the hell knows what really happened. I don't recall having heard the story of the night of the sweet, sweet baby Jesus' conception. Perhaps they glossed over that bit. Possibly an opportunity for a whole genre of erotic fan fiction there.

The simplest way to answer the question of character is to look at the way God described himself (through his purported transcribers), and at what he supposedly did (according to his purported reporters). A number of character traits were identified in bold type in the sections about Genesis and the Ten Commandments.

What sort of man would have some, or, God forbid, all of the following characteristics?

Untrustworthiness - As seen in the series of dirty tricks perpetrated on Adam, Eve and the snake in the Garden of Eden in order to get the whole concept of sin rolling.

Narcissism - Overwhelmingly demonstrated in the first four commandments.

Jealousy - *"I am a jealous and vengeful god..."*

Vindictiveness - Ditto above and illustrated by his decision to punish not only Eve but also the snake, and every single snake and every single woman for all time thereafter. *"...visiting the iniquity of the fathers on the children, and on the third and fourth generations of those who hate Me, but showing mercy to thousands of them that love Me and keep My commandments."*

Control Freak - He makes up rules that he says apply to everybody and threatens wildly disproportionate punishment for ignoring him. Becomes genocidal when disobeyed. Or even when not disobeyed.

Sadism - His decision to make Eve's punishment not a little bit painful, but excruciating. He's the only one capable of witnessing every single act of human childbirth, so he's the only one who could enjoy a sadistic thrill from watching women screaming in pain over and over again.

Misogyny - In addition to the above **sadistic cruelty**, the whole story about Adam's rib and the history of mankind in which all the men were listed by name and the women were ignored.

Hypocrisy - After the event, he behaves as though he didn't want the snake to trick Eve, and he pretends he didn't want Eve to eat from the tree of knowledge. He blatantly blames others for what he deliberately orchestrated. (Now look what you made me do.) Also he uses the tenth commandment to order us not to covet our neighbour's property. Isn't that another way of saying don't be jealous of what someone else has? Yet he openly declared himself to be a jealous guy in the second commandment.

Psychopathic sadism - He could have made humanity simply disappear rather than drowning everybody in the great flood, but he chose the option with the pain and suffering. This is not just a lack of empathy for humanity, but a wilful desire to maximise pain. On many other occasions God doesn't settle for mere killing, he wants those who displease him, aka pretty much everybody, to suffer excruciating pain, forever. So he's not just a bit of a sadist, he's demonstrably the ultimate psychopathic abuser and super sadist of all time. What sort of person would command a man to kill his son as a test? And then actually go and do exactly that by having Jesus, his own son, sort of crucified?

Self-loathing and remorse - After the flood, he promised not to kill everybody again. First he regretted having created so many sinners and then he regretted killing them all.

Capriciousness - How many humans were struck down because God suddenly decided that the city they lived in was evil, or that everybody was evil? And didn't such events occur multiple times after he promised not to kill everyone again?

Megalomania - He didn't like the way the people of Babel were able to co-operate with one another so he scattered them far and wide and made them speak different languages so they would fight each other rather than peacefully co-exist. Possibly the first recorded example of the divide and conquer strategy. (Anyone who prays to this guy for world peace is praying to the wrong god.) That he felt the need to have total control over his creations is also an indication of **self-doubt**. If he wanted unquestioning obedience perhaps he should have just created dogs and given up on the idea of mankind with free will as he was obviously never comfortable with it.

Suspiciousness - East Germany reputedly had as many as one in five citizens operating as informants. Which made life almost intolerable for everybody. God takes that hell on earth scenario and raises the stakes by placing a spy (himself) inside every human brain. A spy that can send you to be tortured in hell for eternity merely for thinking "impure thoughts." Or coveting your neighbour's ass.

The omniscient God concept is a way of saying, "Don't even think about doing anything contrary to my rules because I can read your mind. And I'm always there, listening to your every thought." Making thoughts a crime, courtesy of the tenth commandment, is the work of a **psychotic sadist**. Having created human minds susceptible to jumping all over the place with random thoughts popping in without warning, the big bad **control freak** will now command you not to think about things that your are utterly powerless not to think about. What a prick!

If you think you have control over what you think about, try this - get a watch or stop watch, set it for thirty seconds, and during that thirty seconds do not let your mind think about a dog or a hat or a dog wearing a hat. Go!

How did that go? Couldn't control what you think about? I might just send you to burn in hell. Unless you pray to me every day and grovel and beg forgiveness. Then I might… Until the next time your mind wanders. Under this system the torture begins here on earth. It goes on 24/7. Until you die. And then things get really bad.

Many of the faithful believe that suffering is part of God's plan. Such as the self-flagellators, the cilice-wearers and that famous little witch, Mother Teresa, who it seems deliberately withheld pain medication on the basis that more suffering meant an easier passage to heaven. Either that or she was just a sadist like her God.

So the God created by the mind of mankind, at least the Abrahamic version, is not merely created in man's own image generally, he's created in the image of a man who exhibits the absolute worst of all possible human psychological attributes.

And none of the good attributes.

Forgiveness? Not in Season 1.

Empathy? Totally absent.

Kindness? No.

Generosity? Ha.

Modesty? Get da fuck outta here.

It's claimed that the Old Testament God is loving and caring and kind, but he's not. He's just a psychopath. Telling you he loves you between periods of abuse and alongside threats of eternal punishment isn't love, it's sadism. It's controlling. It's abusive.

As long as the threat is there, that totally wipes out the possibility of any genuine empathy, love or kindness. Those traits can't coexist with such overwhelming psychopathy.

Genuine love, compassion and empathy have no element of threat, fear, power or control. All the so-called love of this God is conditional. Conditional love is not love, it's a bargaining chip. No, not even that, because there's nothing to bargain. There's nothing in it for the human. It's coercion. It's slavery. Do what I say or your punishment will be unimaginably painful and never ending!

And then you're expected to believe that the afterlife will be different. After living a whole lifetime on this planet under conditions of constant mental duress, you'll be blissfully happy forever in heaven.

Fool me once. Get to fuck.

If this God were a human who put you through that amount of shit and then told you to get in the van with no windows because he'll take you somewhere to live happily ever after, would you trust him?

Why would sex and drugs and rock 'n' roll be okay in God's heaven if they're not okay on God's earth?

Why on earth would you trust a guy who made your whole life a mental gulag? Made you feel guilty every time you felt horny. First he gives you sexual desire, then he tells you that feeling horny is bad. Adultery is a sin. Masturbation is a sin. Sexual release is only permitted for married couples and then only for procreation purposes. (I'm not sure if that was actually God or just his priests here on earth with those particularly silly rules, but I don't really care because it's all part of the same bullshit.)

What makes you think someone with character traits like those above will turn into a nice guy in the second half of the game? Why would he make heaven a lovely, relaxing, fun place to be with unlimited free will, free of guilt, free of repercussions, if he could go on controlling and torturing you forever? It's something he obviously enjoys.

And what if heaven turns out to be another Garden of Eden? A place that seems blissful at first but just when you think things are good, God slips on his Joker mask and plays a dirty trick like he did on Adam and Eve. Ha ha. No heaven for you. It's an eternity of suffering instead.

We know how capricious he can be. How merciless. He showed us that he's okay with genocide. He sometimes expressed remorse, but only in the form of self-pity, as he made no attempt to make up for the terror he inflicted on humans. If he truly regretted drowning everybody why didn't he turn back time? But no, even though he's said to exist outside of time and space he is apparently unable to reverse time for any reason. He could sing about wanting to do it, like Cher, but actually do it? Nah.

God - 0 Superman - 1

Is there any example in the Bible where God brings someone back from hell? I don't know. But I doubt it.

It's not hard to imagine the God of the Old Testament as a medieval king who has a childhood friend locked in a dungeon. One day, many years on, the king's brother raises the topic of the guy in dungeon number 43.

Who?

Your old friend. Your best buddy when you were kids. He's been there since he was 12. Don't you think fifteen years is long enough?

Fifteen years in a dungeon? Since he was 12? So how old is he now? 25? 32? Ooooh wee, that is definitely not my idea of fun.

Especially not on bread and water.

No wine? No cheese? That's harsh. Why did I put him there?

They say he beat you at checkers.

Bullshit. Nobody beats the king. Fuck 'im. Let him rot. And who's "they" that said that. Lock them up too.

Of course the problem that arises with such a god/person/spirit/thing is that any organisation led by a despot is going to behave in a despotic manner.

Perhaps not every Nazi was a full blown psychopath. Some may not have enjoyed all of the depraved shit they found themselves having to do, but their leaders laid down rules to ensure they behaved like cruel, racist, pitiless assholes. So they ended up doing it.

Canadian professor Stephen A Kent said that L Ron Hubbard was a malignant narcissist who wrote the rules for Scientology to create an organisation that as a whole behaved like a malignant narcissist. Which it certainly does. There are numerous examples of Scientologists harassing and intimidating those who fail to submit to the rules, stories of families ripped apart by an organisation that claims to do good for the world. (One thing that there's no shortage of in religions is hypocrisy. I'm tempted to elaborate on the evil of this horrific organisation, but this isn't the right place for that. See the TV series made by Leah Remini.)

The Catholic Church engaged in a reign of terror over much of Europe, and parts of the Americas, Asia and Africa for over six hundred years, torturing and killing tens of thousands of people in the name of their God, in the cause of enforcing their God's commandments, for such things as blasphemy, apostasy and heresy.

The Catholic Church didn't stop behaving like a pack of marauding, rabid dogs because of some enlightenment that came over them. They stopped because of the enlightenment that occurred to people outside the church. The Catholic Church throttled back on the despotism only when they no longer had the power to continue to exert their depravity. In public at least. The fact that they continue to get away with abusing their congregation to this day is a ridiculous travesty that is already widely recognised but still hasn't been curtailed.

The only comforting thought regarding all this is that God is a fictional character. A creation of the human brain. The centuries of misery and suffering and death and torture and slaughter all in the name of some stupid shit that someone made up a long time ago, stupid shit that more assholes continue to embellish to this day, is too awful to fully comprehend.

But it's not as bad as the alternative.

If all this nonsense were true we would all be living in a hell from which there is no possible escape. Ever. Not even the escape of death. Not even for the believers. Death would merely be the moment when you understood that the nightmare was never going to end. Either in the Orwellian thought control police state of never-ending heaven, or the physical torture of the flames of a never-ending hell.

The question asked at the start of this section is, what sort of man would have some, or, God forbid, all of the characteristics exhibited by God?

When you compare the God of the Bible to the cruelest, most extreme human despots there is no difference. Except that some despots may have a redeeming feature. Maybe.

Some apologists will point out that the religion they subscribe to is not the religion of that old God, but rather the religion of the God of the New Testament. They say the Jesus third of the God triumvirate is a much kinder, gentler, more empathetic, loving god than God the Father. Fuck! Off! Seriously. Fuck the fuck off. What a cop out. Everybody knows that as long as the patriarch lives, the rules of the patriarch are the rules that count. Ask Rupert Murdoch or Logan Roy if the words of their sons count for anything.

Why did the men who wrote the Bible decide to make the God character such an evil prick? Such a vile despot? Perhaps because so many men in the real world who rise to power are such men. In times gone by a determined psychopathic narcissist had to physically fight his way to power. Now a relentless urge, along with cunning and the willingness to bulldoze behavioural norms may be enough.

The disturbing thing about "strong man" leaders such as Putin, Stalin, Hitler, numerous Popes, Imams and many, many more, is that they have so many fans. Fans for whom the lying, the corruption, the hypocrisy, the cruelty, the violence, the murder and genocide is not a problem, because the evil ways of the despot align with the bigotries and blood lust of their fans.

It seems that the men who wrote the character of God in the Bible were such men. Men who respected a strong ruler. Men who did not respect empathy, or kindness or understanding or a sense of fair play. Or women. Especially women. They wanted to have it written as part of holy law that women were to be servants of men. In every way. Adam's helpers. The scribes were men who wanted to establish strict rules and severe punishment for those who did not agree with them.

They wrote of a God who promised unconditional love, but whose conditions were many. A God who promised Heaven for the faithful, but who slaughtered whole cities if the mood took him. A God whose deceitful actions in the Garden of Eden demonstrated that he could not be trusted, yet who demanded trust in his promise of the sort of happiness in the afterlife that he never showed any hint of allowing on earth.

Thank God he's not real. What a despicable character.

But why was the God of the Bible written as a petty, jealous, violent, sadistic tyrant?

Perhaps because the rulers that have historically wielded the most power have exhibited exactly those qualities and therefore a heavenly ruler would be more plausible that way.

Also because it's much easier to manipulate people when they're afraid. Christians are fond of calling themselves decent, upstanding, God-fearing citizens. They wear that fear like a badge of honour. Most people wouldn't fear a reasonable, compassionate god. But a bully who'll strike you down for picking up sticks on the Sabbath? Uh oh I'd better be careful not to upset him. Pussies.

Mysterious Ways

Whenever there's an obvious contradiction or some other ridiculousness in the Bible, the explanation is that God works in mysterious ways. Mysterious ways is biblical jargon for magic. Or bullshit.

When a story or some action possibly attributable to God makes no sense it may trigger an exhausting bout of apologetics, but in the end it will come down to mysterious ways. If Jesus could feed five thousand people using his mysterious ways, why hasn't God ever done anything about the millions of people who've starved to death over the millennia? Mysterious ways. Oh, okay then, yeah good, fair enough, that explains it.

The most mysterious thing about God's ability to do magic, aka miracles, is that he seems to have given up doing it. Why? Seems a bit mysterious. Perhaps it has something to do with the arrival of cameras and smart phones.

When you trick a cat or dog with some kind of disappearing ball game, the expression on their face tells you that magic is not a satisfying answer. They look confused until they tire of your bullshit, then they look at you like you just farted and walk off.

Mysterious ways is the answer that's designed to shut down the annoying questions of enquiring minds. An answer that's meant to somehow satisfy or suppress the appetite for knowledge, but it's worse than a third of a gopher and more like a picture of a chicken dinner in that it may serve to arouse an appetite but it will have no chance of beddin' 'er back down.

Mysterious ways is the biggest cop out ever invented. Mysterious ways = doesn't make sense = ridiculous bullshit. There is no other meaning.

How does Santa Claus get to every house on earth in one night? Mysterious ways. More bullshit is the only answer when the proposition is bullshit. It's an answer that only makes sense if you believe in magic with a childlike naiveté.

Mysterious ways is invoked when a hurricane or bushfire devastates a town and the only things not destroyed are a few hymn books and bibles and perhaps a crucifix or some other graven image that God would definitely look kindly upon. It's a miracle. God saved his own books while the rest of the town burnt to the ground and people died. Praise the Lord. Seriously. The delusion runs deep.

Although it might be seen to be more than a miracle. It might be God testing the faith of his flock. Which is even better. He's making us suffer for our faith. To see if we're truly worthy of entering his kingdom of heaven when our time comes.

The Gender Reveal Party

Gary and Janice lived in Bokton, a hill town of about six hundred people, an hour or so north of Napa, California. When Janice became pregnant she and Gary got married. When the baby began to show, they, meaning Janice, decided to hold a gender reveal party.

If it was a girl, Gary wanted to call her Kristen, because he liked the sound of the name and he thought it was a nice way to honour Christ. Janice was not so much of a believer, and thought that Kirsten was the correct way to spell that name. It was the sort of thing that might start a silly fight so even though they both felt quite strongly about their preference, they decide to defer that argument in case it was a boy.

Gary's brother Ben said that an identity reveal party might not be a good idea because how would they know which gender the baby would choose to identify as, when it got a bit older. Gary told Ben to keep his stupid ideas to himself. He blamed Ben's wacky thinking on the six months Ben had spent in San Francisco the previous year.

Ben wasn't completely wacky. He phrased it as diplomatically as possible when he suggested that nobody else gave a flying fuck what gender Gary and Janice's baby would be. He was also much too diplomatic to say that a skin colour reveal party after the baby's birth would be more entertaining, as Gary seemed to be the only person in town who was confident about the baby's paternity.

When Janice had first suggested the idea of the reveal party Gary wasn't keen, but after watching YouTube videos of reveal parties gone bad he got quite interested in the idea. Ben thought Gary was kidding when he suggested smoke flares and fireworks. Even an idiot like Gary knew that there were fires ripping through half the state and there was a ban on lighting so much as a joint or a cigarette outdoors unless there was a plentiful water supply within ten feet. Although Gary was an idiot, he knew from Ben's reaction that anybody he asked to help in the planning and execution of the event would try to talk him out of pyrotechnics, so he decided to organise it on his own.

The reveal had to be big. Big meant outdoors. Big meant up in the air. Gary couldn't afford anything attached to a plane or a helicopter so that meant a big thing that could be launched or initiated from the ground. His idea was based on the balloon burst reveal, except that instead of a small party balloon he wanted to use a huge balloon flying on the end of a hundred foot tether.

The huge balloon idea was quickly modified when Gary found a five-pack of 36" black balloons on Amazon for $8.99. Gary planned to fill them with strips of thin plastic which he would cut from plastic shopping bags, also found on Amazon, which came in packs of 180 containing both blue and pink bags for just $17.99. The black balloons carried a warning -

WARNING. Use only Helium. DO NOT USE HYDROGEN! EXPLOSION HAZARD WHEN USING HYDROGEN! DANGER!

Gary smiled. Explosion hazard? Brilliant. He set to work trying to source a bottle of compressed hydrogen.

When the day of the gender reveal party arrived Gary told Janice to stay out of the garage as that was where the reveal device was being loaded. Janice's most sensible and reliable friend had been given the task of finding someone who would not be attending the party to load the appropriate colored plastic strips into the balloons. Gary then applied the gas bottle to the balloons and inflated them. They were tied together and attached to a long coil of nylon cord. Gary double checked all the knots. He'd seen too many balloons fly away on YouTube to make that basic mistake.

A half hour before the guests arrived Gary took the balloons out back and let out the cord so they hovered about fifty feet above the back yard. He tied the cord to a tree and went inside. The cord disappeared into the foliage of the tree and unless someone looked up in that direction, the balloons would wait silently and unnoticed for their moment. Adding to their concealment was a light breeze that held the balloons over the neighbour's yard. He'd have to untie them and walk them back to the house so they flew directly overhead when the time came. The breeze was a blessing in another way as it was a very hot, sunny afternoon. Too hot to be outside without the breeze.

Gary stashed his shotgun under the back steps. He was going to leave it loaded, but then he remembered there'd be children coming so he emptied the gun and put the shells in his pocket.

About half an hour later when all the guests had a drink in hand the moment had arrived. Where was Janice? A couple of her friends went into the house to find her. Right then Gary noticed two kids by the tree. They'd found the cord and were in the process of untying it. Gary dashed towards them, "Noooooooo!" But he was too late. As he reached the tree he and the kids watched the end of the cord disappear up through the foliage.

"Fuck, shit, fuck!" He sprinted back to the house, grabbed his shotgun from under the steps, hurriedly slammed in a couple of shells and took aim at the swiftly receding balloons, not only higher now, but also moving away from the house out over the brush. Boom! Followed immediately by a much louder, BOOM!

Five 36" balloons full of hydrogen make for a massive explosion, enough to rattle the windows of all the nearby houses. Everybody was stunned, including Gary. It was a much bigger bang than he'd anticipated even after all the YouTube research he'd done.

Janice arrived at the back door. "What the fuck was that?" The upturned heads in the yard provided the answer. She'd missed the massive fireball but was still stunned to see what followed. The high temperature meant the air did little to cool the buckshot and half an hour in the hot sun inside the black balloons was enough to superheat the plastic confetti strips and the hydrogen. The explosion was enough to ignite every strip, resulting in a flaming waterfall cascading out of the sky. "Holy shit!" said Janice. "Oh the humanity,"said Ben.

As impressive as the moment was, it was a complete failure in another regard. "What color's that meant to be?" The red and yellow flames completely overwhelmed the colour of the plastic, so nobody was sure of the gender. Some thought they saw some blue, others said red or pink. The display finished as the last of the flaming confetti disappeared into the trees about a quarter mile from the house. Mutterings could be heard referring to what a fucking idiot Gary was, something everybody already knew, but many nevertheless felt the need to reiterate.

There was some laughter as well as disappointment and recrimination, as nobody knew the gender of the baby. The only person who knew had gone home before the guests arrived, and she'd taken the test result with her. Janice hadn't had time to figure out exactly what to do about that when someone shouted, "Fire"!

Sure enough, where the flaming plastic waterfall had landed there was smoke. Lots of it. It was near the edge of town and the wind was blowing away from them, so they were not initially too concerned. But then the wind mysteriously changed direction and the fire rushed into town with the vigour of a shift of thirsty mine workers fresh from a dry fortnight at a mining camp.

Despite their best efforts, the good citizens of Bokton were completely overwhelmed by the fire. Every house was burned to the ground and thirty people died whilst foolishly trying to fight the blaze rather than getting in their trucks and getting the hell out of there. The argument over Kirsten or Kristen would never be required and nobody who attended the party ever had the gender revealed to them as most perished that afternoon, along with Gary and Janice and the never to be pronounced baby.

Ben crashed his truck into a tree whilst trying to avoid a baby deer that ran out of a burning bush into his path. The prayers of thanks to the Lord for saving the life of the baby deer, and the significance of the burning bush were short lived as the fawn had to be put down two days later, although the prayers of thanks for God's miracle at the church were widely reported, especially in the more religiously inclined media outlets. The walls and roof of the church were totally incinerated, but parishioners were able to recover five bibles, three packets of wafers and two cases of communion Zinfandel.

The Lord works in mysterious ways.

What if God's dead?

There aren't degrees of dead. A bit dead, slightly dead, nearly dead, extremely dead, deadish, sort of dead, and almost dead, don't mean dead.

Dead is dead. Something is either dead or not dead.

Although there is perhaps a case to be made for partially dead. A tree can have branches that are dead, and therefore be partially dead but once the whole tree is dead, then it's dead. A mountain climber or polar explorer can have fingers and toes turn black with frostbite, which is a similar thing. If you don't prune the deadwood then the dead spreads, baby, the dead spreads. If you cut off a healthy finger with an axe, then it will be dead fairly soon unless there's someone handy to stitch it back on. If your finger remains apart, then it will soon be dead, but that wouldn't make you partially dead. You'd still be alive, just a bit lighter.

And there's no temporarily dead. There is no such thing as rising from the dead. It's right there in the definition of the word dead - "The permanent cessation of vital functions." Returning from the dead just means that the cessation of vital functions was not permanent. Meaning death did not occur.

A near-death experience means that someone was nearly dead. But not quite. Unless they died. In which case they became dead. Forever.

Since the events described in the Bible about the life and times of God and his boy Jesus during their foray into our time and space over two thousand years ago, there have been no confirmed sightings of either of them. Or their sidekick, the Holy Ghost.

There have been lots of TV shows about ghosts, but not the holy one, and in fact I don't even know what he's meant to look like. He's sometimes represented in religious art as a dove, but that's more like a placeholder. Why the fuck would the holy ghost look like a dove? Why not a cow? If he's part of the holy trinity wouldn't he also be a long-haired bearded, man? Nah, then heaven would look like a ZZ Top concert. Anyway...

The lack of any sightings, or signs, let alone vital signs, would seem to be a reasonable argument for claiming that God is in fact dead. And always has been, given the lack of solid evidence from any time in history.

Maybe God was kind of like a celestial squid that died upon spawning the Big Bang, turning himself into stardust in the process. What? There's crazier shit than that in the Bible. Well, just as crazy.

Everyone's free to make up their own theory of course, though it's probably safer not to. Whatever implausible fantasy someone comes up with, someone else will believe it, preach it and then gullible people will have yet another thing to fight about.

Since the invention of video cameras, God has never been seen, never been heard, never performed a miracle, never done anything to establish his existence. Which is the same behaviour exhibited by dead people. God is the same, in every measurable way, as an old donkey that was burnt to a crisp in a barn fire a thousand years ago.

If there is no way to describe, in any measurable way, the difference between two things, there is no basis on which to claim they are different. God is as dead as that dead donkey. And just as imaginary.

Were he not dead, the God that decreed the Ten Commandments would surely object to the contents of this book, and his omnipotence could easily cause it to cease to exist. He'd probably drown it. Or turn it into a pillar of salt. But no. He does nothing. Every day. Nothing. Not a peep out of him. About anything. Ever. Nothing. Like a dead thing.

Ergo, God is dead. Does not exist and never has.

God's Judgement Day

Faithful followers of God are forever banging on about Judgement Day. The day we die. The day God judges us. The day that we are supposed to fear so much that we regularly bow down and give money to charlatans. It seems a little one-sided. For balance, perhaps we should have an opportunity to judge God. There's no point in waiting until God's Judgement Day because then we'll be dead, so we should get on with it before that happens.

Like Michelangelo's *Creation of Adam*, God's Judgement Day is ambiguous. It can mean the day that God does the judging or the day that God is judged.

If God created man then what it says in the bible stands. But if man created God, then it is incumbent on man to judge God, if only for quality control reasons.

Using the second meaning for God's Judgement Day, how should we judge God? What would be suitable criteria for God's Judgement Day? Well, he'll presumably judge us according to his rules as written in his big black book, so let's start there.

The most important of God's rules must surely be his Ten Commandments. The Ten Commandments are not only what God considers to be the most important rules for humans to live by, they're also a statement of God's intent, his most fervent desires for himself.

When judged according to his own Ten Commandments, the God of the Bible is an abject failure.

Here's why.

God's first commandment, his number one desire, was for him to be the one god, the only god. That hasn't happened. In addition to the millions of people who don't worship any god, there are many millions more who have worshipped thousands of different gods over the years. Gods come and go like fashion trends. Gods are nowhere near uncommon, let alone unique. Complete fail.

The second commandment was that no images were to be created, no likenesses or symbols for people to worship. That hasn't happened. (People who ignore him completely don't even realise they're accidentally complying.) People who do pray to God have flouted that rule by bowing down and praying before images of Jesus being killed. Nice. They wear these images around their necks and hang them on bedroom walls. What do they think the second commandment means? It's a mystery.

His third wish was to enforce blasphemy laws that would punish those who took his name in vain. Hashtag OMG. Hashtag JFC. So that hasn't happened either. Expletives utilising heavenly creatures are as common as those involving body parts and sexual acts. Blasphemy laws are sometimes enforced in barbaric places where women are still stoned to death in the name of "honour" and for other imagined sins. Places where the word of God is most strictly obeyed, the places most likely to feel like hell on earth.

God's fourth most important desire was for everybody to keep one day aside purely for worshipping him. That hasn't happened. Even in devout Christian communities the worship lasts for an hour or two, then they get on with sport and shopping, if they themselves don't have to go to work. Mostly God's desired day of rest and praise is ignored.

His fifth demand was for people to honour their parents. The only places where that one gets enforced are the same places where people get stoned to death. People with reasonable parents don't need this rule as it happens naturally. Good parents are loved by their children. It would only need to be enforced when children had been maltreated or abused in some way. Sold as sex slaves perhaps. Hell of a rule.

On the second stone tablet, God commanded all humans not to kill, steal, commit adultery, bear false witness or covet other people's stuff. Given the subject matter of most news stories every single day, those last five commandments are also not being followed according to God's directives. How can a God be said to be all-powerful if all of his commands are routinely ignored, mostly without consequence?

Once upon a time God supposedly drowned every human on the planet except for Noah and family, because they weren't behaving in a way that pleased him. There doesn't seem to be a definitive consensus on the dates or chronology of events in the Old Testament but perhaps a thousand years or so after the great drowning God gave the tablets to Moses. That was possibly one to two thousand years before the nailing of the Jesus.

So the deliberately vague storyline is that God created man, dabbled with his experiment for one or two thousand years, drowned everybody, dabbled less often for a thousand or so years more, produced his ten commandments, and has, ever since, watched over a planet where all his most important desires are pissed all over every single day. And he hasn't done a damn thing about it for at least three and a half thousand years. Unless you count that stunt where he pretended that Jesus died, but only the faithful would rate that as a success, even if it had actually happened.

What was the point of Jesus anyway?

1 Timothy 1:15 CEV - "Christ Jesus came into the world to save sinners."

1 Corinthians 15:3 CEV - "Christ died for our sins."

Is it the singer or the song? The sinners or the sins?

Did Timmy mean that Jesus came into the world to save all those who were sinners up to that point, or all sinners for all time? If it's the former, just those who had already sinned, then does that mean all those early sinners, the saved ones, are in heaven? Are there Neanderthals in Heaven?

If it's the latter then that means all of us. We're all sinners according to the holy rollers, so did Jesus' mission ensure that we all go to heaven without needing to pray every day or every week? The Bible bashers would say no. You must believe and pray. Well, if it doesn't mean we get a free admission ticket, then how are we saved? What are we saved from, if not hell? Why die for our sins if it makes no difference to the heaven admission process? If it makes no difference to anything?

Where did sin come from? The Garden of Eden. If God hadn't done his dirty tricks back there, there'd be no sin and no need for Jesus. God created the problem, and then arranged for the torture and execution of his only begotten son to solve the problem. But the world is still full of sin to this day, at least according to God's priests. Well done, God. Great display of omnipotence. Frank Spencer could only stand back in admiration.

The more you look at this stuff the more likely you are to slither down a rabbit hole of apologetics, semantics, polemics and theological nonsense, so we'll just leave the Jesus mission there. It's all ridiculous bullshit anyway.

What is clear is that ever since there's been some sort of reliable historical record, the omnipotent one has been impotent, the omniscient one may as well have been blind, and the omnipresent one has never been seen. At least not by any sane person.

So there it is. God's Judgement Day.

Out of ten? Zero.

Absolute fail.

Penultimate Brainfarts

One day we might discover something amazing regarding the universe, the meaning of life or a higher power or spiritual being. We may find proof that we're all characters in a computer simulation. These things must remain a possibility, however remote, until all the questions are answered.

But making shit up does not provide an answer to anything. It just obfuscates and makes us all less intelligent.

Even if you firmly believe you have spoken with God or vice versa, it's far more likely to be imagination than reality. We know this because thousands of people have had such experiences but never has the existence of any sort of God been proven. Never.

If it had been, we'd have all heard about it.

It would be the biggest news event of all time.

There'd be no more argument.

The fact that we haven't heard about any irrefutable proof of the existence of any God, is itself proof that proof of the existence of God has never been found.

Religious believers look around and declare that the universe itself is evidence of the existence of God, because where else could all this wonderful stuff have come from?

Only God could've created something this magnificent. The problem with claiming God created everything is that it doesn't answer where God came from. Outside of time and space is a concept that is beyond our genuine comprehension. It comes from the ancient art of woo-woo, which is the theory of stringing together words that sound impressive but actually mean nothing. We may imagine what it means, just as we may imagine a God who has always existed. But that's the only place those things exist. In the imagination.

Whilst religious believers can't adequately answer the question of where God came from, the human imagination is not only a plausible answer, it's the only plausible answer.

Conclusion

If… God was created by the human brain…

Then…. Whoever created the God of the Bible did a really crappy job.

The creators of God chose, as a role model, the image of the type of man who sadly, and far too often, rises to power - a violent, vain, capricious, sadistic sociopath who demands total subservience and promises only lies that can never be substantiated.

There were lots of big claims - omnipotence, omniscience, omnipresence and unconditional love, but there's no evidence for any of that. Not in the real world, and not in the Bible. In fact, the Bible has numerous examples of the shortcomings of God.

The God of the old testament is a jealous, vindictive asshole. He says so himself. He's also a genocidal maniac who killed more humans than all the despots, dictators, psychopaths and serial killers in history put together. (And he made them too, if you believe that shit, so he's also responsible for everything they did and continue to do.) And because his grand plan makes him responsible for everything on earth, the suffering he's inflicted due to poverty and hunger and disease and drought and famine and hurricanes and tornadoes and earthquakes and volcanoes is so immense as to be unimaginable. And immeasurable.

It's a good thing that God is a fictional character, created, however poorly, by the human brain.

Life's tough enough without a bastard like him lurking about.

If... the human brain was created by God...

Then... God did a really crappy job.

According to God himself. He was never satisfied with us and kept killing everyone and starting over. Because we're all sinners. Unless we bow down before him every day. Or at least every seventh day, though that might not be enough for the guy who invented hell just for us.

As outlined in the preceding chapters, the human brain has more negative features than positive ones. We're vain, jealous, greedy, violent, short-tempered and vindictive (as well as sometimes being kind and generous and clever and all that good stuff). When we take a wide look at the world and the way we live in it, meaning the societies and communities we've created, most of them have a lot of problems. A lot of them are truly terrible.

If God's plan was to make this world a decent place for humans to live, then his programming of the human brain was woeful.

Regarded as things that were designed, God and the Human Brain are both examples of Not Very Intelligent Design.

However, as an organ in an organism that evolved from a single cell a long time ago, the human brain is astonishing. Truly magnificent. Worthy of awe. Almost unbelievable. Except it is believable because all other explanations are simply not credible.

The best thing about the human brain is that it allows us to love. To be part of a family, or a group of friends. This life would be almost unbearable if we had to go through it with no real connection to others. Some connections may be to someone we don't know, and the connection is because of something they wrote, or sang, or painted, or filmed, and that is what makes us feel a connection, as though we belong, and we share an understanding. That this earth is our home and we have a place in this home. All our foibles, our craziness and the silly things we do and believe, we can understand of each other, and we can forgive each other for our human frailties and love each other despite our shortcomings.

The human brain allows us to revel in the beauty of it all.

The End

For more stuff by Neel Ingman,

check out

neelingman.com

or go to

youtube.com/@neelingman

Thanks for reading

Reviews are the best way to help other readers find books they'll enjoy.

A brief review, just a sentence or two, will let other readers know what you liked about the book, and why you think they may like it too.

So if you enjoyed this book please leave a review or at least a rating at Amazon.com or Goodreads.com or anywhere else that you can.

And PLEASE DO IT RIGHT NOW before you forget (you know you will).

If you'd like to be notified of new books by Neel Ingman please sign up to the mailing list at neelingman.com

Cheers, Neel